THE COLLABORATIVE
MATH CLASSROOM

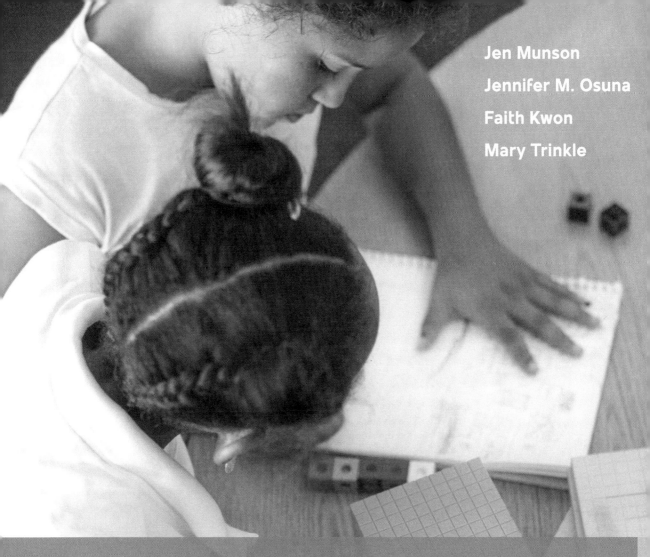

Jen Munson
Jennifer M. Osuna
Faith Kwon
Mary Trinkle

THE COLLABORATIVE MATH CLASSROOM

Launching a Student-Centered Mathematical Community

HEINEMANN
Portsmouth, NH

Heinemann

145 Maplewood Avenue, Suite 300

Portsmouth, NH 03801

www.heinemann.com

ISBN-13: 978-0-325-13254-9

Library of Congress Control Number: 2022950637

Editor: Katherine Bryant

Production: Victoria Merecki, Sonja Chapman

Cover design: Suzanne Heiser

Interior design: Shawn Girsberger

Cover and interior photos: Lauren Audet, Sherry Day, and Michael Grover

Typesetting: Shawn Girsberger

Manufacturing: Val Cooper

Printed in the United States of America on acid-free paper.

1 2 3 4 5 VP 27 26 25 24 23   PO 4500866169

Contents

5   PHASE 4: Becoming a Student-Led Mathematics Community   105

Acknowledgments

To say that writing this book was a collaborative effort would seem obvious, and yet it took a team far larger than the four of us to make it possible. We are deeply indebted to the children from whom we have learned about mathematics collaboration, both in our own classrooms and in the classrooms of gracious teachers who have opened their doors so that we might learn. We thank them—children and teachers alike—for their willingness to be brave and try new things, for inviting us into their thinking and collaborations, and for their enthusiasm, curiosity, and brilliance. In particular, we would like to thank Ruby Dellamano, Alissa Fong, Raha Haghnia, Cindy Hill, Geetha Lakshminarayanan, Thomas Rodney, and all the other classroom teachers and coaches who inspired and nourished the work represented here.

Our thinking about collaboration, equity, authority, and classroom discourse has been fed by the scholarship and writing of many, including Deborah Ball, Paul Cobb, Randi Engle, Cathy Fosnot, Megan Franke, Michael Fried, Beth Herbel-Eisenmann, Cathy Humphreys, Elham Kazemi, Magdalene Lampert, Rachel Lotan, Judit Moschkovich, Peg Smith, Mary Kay Stein, and Tracy Zager.

Many thanks to the indefatigable Katherine Bryant for her role in shaping this book from the start. Finally, we wish to thank our families for their support over the many years it took to mull over, talk about, and write this book: Benny, Baby Hani, Bre, Dave, Gabriel, Sofia, Ash, and Ruby. Through a pandemic and life changes and simply growing up a little every day, we couldn't have done it without you.

Introduction

Joel and Filemu sat on the carpet in one corner of the classroom surrounded by shelves of books and tools trying to decide what to do next. Their second-grade class had been asked to figure out how many T-shirts were left in their class's imagined T-shirt factory inventory. Joel and Filemu were in charge of the medium T-shirts. On the previous day they had 56 medium T-shirts in inventory, and today they were told that 37 of these T-shirts had been sold. How many medium T-shirts remained? Joel said to Filemu, "That's a lot. I don't know," and seemed to be stumped as they both stared at the problem. Filemu then erupted with an idea, "I know! Let's use cubes!" Joel's face softened, and with a "Yeah!," he hopped up to get a basket of snap cubes from the shelf behind them.

Joel suggested they make sticks of 10 cubes each, something they had done before, but Filemu was suddenly concerned. "But we only need 5 sticks of 10. It won't be fair," she said, as she noticed that one of them would get to make 2 sticks of 10 while the other would make 3. This was a serious problem for Filemu, but Joel pointed out that someone had to make the 6 extras to show fifty-*six*, not just fifty, T-shirts. Satisfied, they made their model, and then decided to act out selling the T-shirts. Joel would buy them from Filemu, and they would see how many they had left. Filemu immediately handed over 30 T-shirts, in the form of 3 sticks of 10 cubes, and then the pair faced the conundrum of how best to act out selling 7 more shirts from their remaining 26 T-shirts. They stared at the sticks of 10 and the 6 loose cubes. "What could we do?" Filemu asked Joel.

These two second graders had been working together for ten minutes and had already navigated several hurdles. They decided how to get started on solving the problem before them by agreeing on a tool to model the situation. They decided how to use that tool in a way that reflected and leveraged their understanding of base ten. They figured out how each of them could contribute equally to creating the model. And they decided to act out the action of the story to model selling T-shirts. When they confronted yet one more conceptual dilemma, Filemu turned not to their teacher, but to her partner to generate an idea of what to do next. This is complex work for a pair of seven-year-olds, but it is precisely the kind of work that leads to deep mathematical learning.

Learning Mathematics Is Fundamentally Social

The study of human learning and development is clear: learning is a social endeavor. We have long known that we learn by exploring and reflecting on our world with one another (Dewey 1985 [1916]). People learn through interaction with our environment, with one another, and, in this case, with the discipline of mathematics (National Academies of Sciences, Engineering, and Medicine 2018; National Research Council 1999). And yet, peek into the typical classroom and you are likely to see individual seats in clean rows, with students often working on assignments on their own with little talk allowed or encouraged. What a wasted opportunity to engage the curiosity of so many humans in the room! Why?

To put it plainly, it is harder to foster collaboration and inquiry and make sense of students' complex mathematical thinking than it is to put students in rows and ask for simple right and wrong answers. Although the former offers the possibility of greater engagement, more robust learning, deeper connection, and even joy, the latter is alluring because it is an environment that is easier to control. But it goes against what we know about how humans learn and, in practice, acts as a factory model that produces many students who dislike, avoid, and do not understand math. The results from the 2017 National Assessment of Educational Progress (NAEP) showed that only 34 percent of eighth-grade students performed at or above the Proficient level on the mathematics assessment. Fully half of Americans experience math anxiety (Boaler 2012); ask around and you are likely to hear fully competent adults claim that they are no good in math and often quite phobic of it.

In contrast, collaborative and cooperative approaches to learning mathematics that center reasoning and reflection are effective, engaging, and equitable for students, though ambitious work for teachers. It is worth putting in the hard work of creating a collaborative math classroom, full of mathematical inquiry and reflection, and in this book we will walk you through the steps of how to create one with and for your students.

Shifting Our Role

Engaging in mathematical practices as a classroom and making sense of ideas together requires intellectual risk-taking, creativity, and lots of talk. The National Council of Teachers of Mathematics has been calling for just such a vision since 1989, with the Common Core State Standards jumping on board this train in 2010. And yet, moving toward creating math classrooms like this has been slow and difficult work. Shifting instructional practice means shifting our sense of what it means to teach mathematics well. For example, traditionally, the primary role of the teacher is to explain mathematics (Amit and Fried 2005). In the collaborative classroom, the teacher still explains mathematics, but that role becomes a secondary one, used judiciously in service of a new primary role—to cultivate mathematical inquiry and orchestrate mathematical discussions among students themselves (Herbel-Eisenmann, Wagner, and Cortes 2010; Stein et al. 2008).

When teachers shift roles toward supporting and orchestrating collaborative mathematics experiences among students, they also hand over more of the thinking work to students. Students take on the authority to author and evaluate mathematical ideas. During small-group or partner work, students take on even more of the thinking work since they are largely on their own while the teacher moves from group to group. Students also claim greater agency in how they participate in classroom tasks: they think about mathematics problems in different ways, and all of their ideas might be at play as students make sense of them together.

This can feel messy and complicated. Many interactions happen simultaneously and in a multitude of ways every minute. Control is no longer at the center of classroom management; instead, teachers and students create a particular kind of mathematical community together. It can be dizzying; so much so that it may seem easier to just put kids in rows or ask each student to complete their own worksheet. But we know this is not how people learn effectively.

How We Can Collaborate

In this book, we make five assumptions about you, our reader, and our role as teachers, researchers, professional developers, and writers in supporting your professional learning:

1. You are a professional.
2. You have knowledge that we don't.
3. We want to partner with you on your goals for your classroom and students.

4. Our experiences teaching in, learning from, and researching collaborative classrooms could support you in your journey.

5. We don't have all the answers. This is messy, beautiful work.

This means that we know that our experiences are not a mirror of yours, and therefore you may find that *your* collaborative math classroom looks different from the examples we describe in this book. Your journey to that classroom may have bumps and wiggles that echo ours but are specific to your context. And your deep knowledge of your students and context, along with the resources you have available, and understanding your own comfort zone are going to be critical to crafting a collaborative classroom. In this book, we draw on our collective experiences and expertise, and we, too, are learning all the time—from one another and from students—what it means to learn math together in community. If you want to launch a collaborative math classroom, but you're not sure how to wade into all this messiness productively and equitably, we can help. If you're a coach or administrator trying to promote school-wide change, we hope this book can break down the challenges into more manageable stages that you and your teams can think through together. Wherever you are, we invite you to join us.

How This Book Is Structured

We begin with setting a vision of teaching and learning mathematics and the principles that drive a collaborative mathematics classroom (Chapter 1). Since every classroom and context is different, we have designed the heart of this book around a set of goals, rather than as a series of steps. We know that no fixed set of rules, no formula, would ever work in every context. Indeed, having created collaborative classrooms again and again, we know that each group of children can require something different from us. But we have found that even with all these differences, some core goals guide us each year, and those goals tend to unfold in phases. This book is structured around four such phases (see Chapters 2–5). We begin with the premise that you might be starting this work at the beginning of a school year, and so you'll see that planning for your launch is the first of these phases (see Chapter 2). However, you can reimagine your math classroom at any point in the year. So, if it is February, and you have decided to dive in, we welcome you. From there, we examine three phases of working with students to establish and grow your collaborative mathematical community: establishing a collaborative structure (Chapter 3), building and sharing authority (Chapter 4), and becoming a student-led mathematics community (Chapter 5).

Just as establishing a collaborative math classroom rolls out in phases, your reading can as well. We encourage you to read the first three chapters of this book as you begin to map out your vision and first steps and not yet get bogged down in what comes after. When you have gotten your classroom launched, you'll want to read more. You're a professional and you'll know when you've read just enough to get started and not so much that you feel daunted. We close Chapters 3, 4, and 5 with signs to celebrate in your class-room—signs that we sometimes overlook—and situations and questions that often arise at that phase. We want to be there with you as you do this work, so try some things in your class and come back to us when we can support you.

The final chapters of this book can be of particular use as you think through issues that come up when you are working on developing a new kind of community. In Chapter 6, we discuss what it means to maintain and sustain a collaborative community over an entire year. In Chapter 7, we grapple with the challenges teachers sometimes face when trying to share authority with their students. And in Chapter 8, we explore how you can communicate with and cultivate support from stakeholders, including parents, colleagues, and school leaders.

Throughout the book, you'll find vignettes from our real classrooms and notes from mathematics education research that we think you will find illuminating and useful in your work. Each is intended to offer yet another way to understand what it means to work together with students to do and learn mathematics.

Meet the Authors

As educators our stance is that all students deserve to have access to quality instruction that centers them as whole humans through an ethic of care and recognition that their identities and experiences are important aspects of learning. We recognize that racism, sexism, and other oppressive ideologies impact how students experience care and recognition in math class, and we hope to offer support with how to empower all students as mathematical thinkers and learners. The four of us have been collaborating as professionals on creating and learning from collaborative elementary mathematics classrooms for six years, each of us in a different role and all of us in constant, ongoing conversation. In this book, you'll hear different voices when we want to draw attention to the different roles we have played, whether as teachers, researchers, or coaches.

Jen Munson

I am currently an assistant professor of learning sciences at Northwestern University, where my research focuses on how interactions support learning in the elementary mathematics classroom. I am particularly interested in how teachers interact with students during collaborative problem-solving and how teachers and math coaches collaborate in the classroom to support teacher learning. Previously, I worked as an elementary and middle school classroom teacher and then as a math coach in Pre-K through eighth-grade classrooms, supporting teachers to foster equitable, productive math classrooms. Spending time in hundreds of classrooms over the years, I learned much from teachers and children about what was possible, and I still had many, many questions. These questions led me to my graduate work at Stanford University, where I worked with Jenny and we met Faith and Mary. Together, we have been learning from what happened in their classrooms as they did the messy and joyful work of sharing authority with their young students, learning we hope to share with you in this book.

Jennifer M. Osuna

I am an associate professor of education at Stanford University. My research focuses on student identity formation in collaborative mathematics classrooms. In particular, my research examines how students work together in whole-class discussions, small-group work, and partner work, examining how they negotiate participation and its effects on how they come to see themselves and others as learners and doers of mathematics. I serve as principal investigator to the research study that housed this writing team, and I led a research group that partnered with five elementary school teachers interested in learning to teach mathematics through collaborative learning activities. Faith and Mary were two of the teachers we partnered with at the time, and their powerful instructional practices were foundational to what our team learned about inclusive, productive, and thriving collaborative mathematics classrooms for young learners.

Faith Kwon

I am a doctoral student at Stanford University, studying race, inequality, and language in education, teacher education, and math education. My research interests include humanizing support for preservice and inservice teachers, particularly for teachers with marginalized identities and justice commitments. Prior to beginning my doctoral studies, I was a first- and second-grade teacher, and a district instructional coach and professional developer supporting early career teachers in developing student-centered, inquiry-based instructional practices. Mary is a longtime colleague and thought partner in the work of building classroom spaces of mathematical collaboration, an inquiry that was hugely supported by Jenny and Jen in my years as a classroom teacher and now graduate student and researcher.

Mary Trinkle

I serve as the elementary math coach for my school district, where I facilitate a program with cohorts of teachers who participate in professional development and coaching to implement collaborative math classrooms. I strive to create trusting and collaborative relationships with teachers and leaders to best support growing teacher practice in ways that center adult learning and the process it takes to be vulnerable in learning. Before this, I taught fourth grade and kindergarten, mostly the former. As a classroom teacher, my ultimate goal was to cultivate a learning environment that centered student inquiry and exploration. My work with Jenny, Jen, and Faith has been essential to my growth, first as a classroom teacher when we met and now as a coach. Our conversations and collaboration have been instrumental to my understanding and implementation of collaborative math classrooms and facilitating professional learning with teachers.

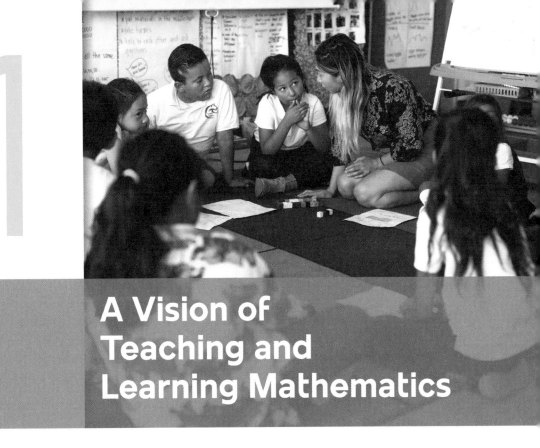

1

A Vision of Teaching and Learning Mathematics

Notes from the Classroom

Let's begin our journey by peeking into Faith and Mary's thinking about their former classrooms, a first- and fourth-grade classroom, respectively, where students learned to work on mathematics together in ways that centered collaboration, mutuality, and self-direction.

FAITH: "What Does It Look Like? What Does It Sound Like?"

Back from recess, my students gather in a circle on the rug, some of them stopping by their tables to hang their sweater or taking a quick drink at the sink on their way. There is a low buzz as they settle; I smile and acknowledge their excitement, then begin by collectively reviewing what we already know about "collaborating" ("working together"), because we will need to collaborate ("work together!") to play our new game. We ask ourselves, "What does it look like when we're collaborating?" and "What does it sound like?" After some think time and one or two initial responses, I point to our anchor chart and other visuals as cues, knowing that eventually they will be able to cue each other and remind themselves how we collaborate and play games together. In a fishbowl, I model the game with a student, simultaneously prompting the students in the circle around us to revoice the steps. I ask if a partnership can model for all of us what it looks like to get started. As Jimena and Eva get up and begin the work of choosing a good spot to work, gathering tools and materials for the game, and negotiating who goes first, I am voicing over their actions and directing the students' attention to the moves they are making as collaborators and mathematicians.

The students indicate with a thumbs up that they are ready to begin this work as well, and I invite them to get started. As this is happening, I am also taking quick scans of the room, taking note of things I may want to bring up as we debrief our game time, but also glimmers of how I know this time will look and sound with time, intentionality, and practice. They may not all be collaborating productively yet, but with repetition, reminders, and a shared vision of how we work together, I know that's where we'll land.

MARY: Buzzing with Collaboration

Looking around my classroom in March, I saw students engaged in their math work the way that I had envisioned in August. Partners were spread across the room, some sitting at tables, leaning in and pointing to each other's work, and some lying on the carpet with manipulatives all around them and with a thinking expression as their partner explained how the materials related to the fraction problem about sandwiches. A few students stood around the board to reread the problem, pausing after each sentence to discuss the context. A student stared out the window and then looked at their work with an excited expression. I could feel in my body that amazing things were happening. I stood there for several moments to soak it in.

In the moment, I decided we would debrief how collaboration was going. I wanted my students to revel in their success. I called for a cleanup and we gathered around the carpet. I asked students, "How did your partnerships go today?" the same way that I had so many times this year. But today was different. One student shared about changing their strategy after seeing what their partner did; another student shared about getting two different answers and having to think through what to do next together; another student shared about a conflict that they had about where to sit and reflected on what might be a better way to solve their problem tomorrow. My students were not only being productive in their partnerships, they were talking about the mathematical work they had done. They connected the work of collaboration to their mathematical thinking. We had reached the magical moment where everything clicked and the classroom was buzzing with collaboration!

A Vision of Teaching and Learning Mathematics

When we imagine a mathematics classroom, certain elements are likely to come to mind: a teacher at the front of the room presenting and explaining procedures, students raising their hands if they have a question or to share the right answer on individual assignments. In this book, we offer an alternative vision for a collaborative mathematics classroom. The role of the teacher is not so much to explain as it is to curate and facilitate rich mathematical experiences that students engage in with one another. Students' mathematical thinking and curiosities drive the day's work; teachers elicit, probe, and help to nudge students' thinking, wonder along with students, and help to create a classroom where students feel seen and heard as mathematical thinkers, learners, and community members. In this vision, the classroom is more than a place where students acquire important content knowledge about mathematics; instead, it is a place of both

learning and becoming. Rather than simply learning mathematics, students learn to become young mathematicians together—posing and making sense of problems, directing their work together, and experiencing themselves and one another as mathematical contributors and thinkers.

A collaborative elementary mathematics classroom is an active, lively, and often joyful place marked by particular kinds of social interaction: children move about the room, finding and using the tools they need to make sense of the ideas at play, whether counting cubes, rulers, base ten blocks, or just paper and markers. Students sit in twos, threes, and fours at tables or sprawled on the rug, discussing strategies for solving problems. You might find it hard to spot the teacher; she's kneeling next to a pair of students as they build ten-sticks with cubes and talking with them about their work, clarifying and nudging their thinking forward.

Realizing this vision of a collaborative classroom might seem overwhelmingly complex at first glance, but we can break this vision down in terms of specific kinds of important social interactions. Social interactions are the building blocks of human activity, including the doing and learning of math. How students interact with the classroom space (the *environment*), with *one another*, and with *mathematics* defines the classroom community and each person's part in it. Rather than a classroom made up of students working on individual assignments or listening to a teacher's explanation, a collaborative classroom involves a variety of peer interactions, including asking questions, explaining ideas, expressing and resolving disagreements, gaining attention, making decisions together, and many more. In other words, unlike a traditional mathematics classroom, a collaborative classroom involves *dialogue.* Opportunities for making sense of mathematics, as well as for identifying positively as a young mathematician, emerge through that dialogue, both in the whole class and small groups. In this sense, collaborative mathematics classrooms can be thought of in terms of particular kinds of social interactions that support student-directed mathematical explorations and dialogue. In this book, we break down collaborative classrooms into their component building blocks and offer detailed and actionable goals to support you in creating such a classroom for you and your students. First, we'll identify some underlying principles to guide our work.

Seven Principles of a Collaborative Mathematics Classroom

We've identified seven principles to guide a collaborative mathematics classroom. In this section we'll highlight each principle and some of the research it is based on.

1. Teachers trust students and themselves. Students trust themselves, each other, and the teacher.

A thriving and productive collaborative classroom is fundamentally built on trust. Teachers must trust that students are earnest in their efforts to engage with the environment, each other, and mathematics. And teachers must also learn to trust themselves by leaning into their curiosity, getting to know their students, responding to students' ideas, and recognizing that not everything needs to go perfectly each day. Students must be able to trust that their teacher will both accept them as they are and guide them in learning how to participate in community with others, that they do have ideas that are worth bringing to their classroom community, and that their peers will respond to their ideas in ways that make them feel seen and heard.

Research Note Understanding Off-Task Activity. Students are earnest participants in classroom activity, even when it seems that they are off task. In a study of the functions of off-task activity on mathematical collaborations, researchers found that most instances of off-task activity actually promoted the collaboration. For example, off-task activity helped a student struggling to contribute to a collaborative work gain the attention of peers and join the collaboration; off-task activity also helped to recruit students into collaboration, to warm up to the work by connecting students, and to resist becoming overpowered by others (Langer-Osuna et al. 2020). Teachers who had the opportunity to attend to and notice the functions of such social negotiations during collaborative mathematics tasks shifted their interpretive lens for making sense of and responding to student behavior, noticing that students were earnest in their attempts to connect with one another and to get on the same page about the task at hand and that teachers could trust those efforts (Langer-Osuna and Munson, under review).

2. Students feel safe to bring their whole selves to doing and learning mathematics.

Trust begets both a sense of agency and a sense of safety. Students feel they can bring their whole selves, including their interests, ideas, curiosities, and experiences, to investigating mathematics with their peers. Sharing one's thinking and wonderings with others takes vulnerability, and, in a space of safety, such willingness to share and contribute fosters rich, productive discussions about the big ideas of mathematics.

Research Note Autonomy and Identity in Math Classrooms. A yearlong case study of student engagement in a collaborative mathematics classroom found that in a classroom where students had a great deal of autonomy in choosing their classroom participation, and where accountability practices were grounded in student-led negotiations, students were able to bring in valued identities to their mathematical work, increasing engagement and the formation of a positive mathematical identity (Langer-Osuna 2015).

3. All student voices are worthy.

A collaborative classroom needs diverse ideas to promote the authentic explorations, discussions, debates, and dilemmas that promote deep understanding. Even incorrect ideas can spark

Research Note Collaboration Supports Inclusion. Decades of research in complex instruction (Cohen and Lotan 2014; Featherstone et al. 2011) have shown the value of mathematical group work structured to support inclusive participation by all students. Cobb (1995) termed this structure as multivocal, and showed that, in multivocal small-group configurations, students engaged in more productive exchanges. Research by Mercer and colleagues (Mercer and Howe 2012; Mercer, Wegerif, and Dawes 1999) has similarly found that multivocality, central to classroom dialogue, helps students to reach greater learning gains.

aha moments when students wrestle with them while considering other ideas. Further, classrooms, when seen as spaces of becoming, require students to learn to use their voice, to explore and practice voicing their own ideas, and to know that their ideas are always worth considering.

4. Teachers center the needs and voices of vulnerable students.

Research Note **Centering the Voices of Marginalized Students.** In a yearlong case study of a collaborative mathematics classroom, Langer-Osuna (2011) found that students' interpretations of and responses to a peer's directives during collaborative work were shaped by gender, ultimately marginalizing the female group leader, while further centering the male group leader. Turner and colleagues (2013) examined a classroom whose participation structures for whole-class discussion explicitly centered marginalized students—in particular, English learners. By centering English language learners through norms such as inviting Spanish language, relying on the classroom community to serve as translators, and expecting monolingual English speakers to attend to and work to make sense of Spanish language contributions, the teacher helped to foster robust and inclusive dialogue.

To have authentic dialogue, students must learn to share intellectual authority to voice and discuss mathematical ideas jointly. Particular students might struggle to be seen and heard in the classroom for a variety of reasons, ranging from issues of status to cultural and social identities to challenges related to attention deficit hyperactivity disorder, autism spectrum disorder, or trauma. By centering the needs and voices of vulnerable students, the classroom creates the space for more inclusive dynamics that ultimately support richer mathematical dialogue.

5. Mathematics focuses on reasoning, sensemaking, and big mathematical ideas.

Students in collaborative math classrooms make sense of mathematics. By exploring and investigating big ideas, such as place value, addition and subtraction, fractions, or shapes, students have the opportunity to reason with one another and develop conceptual understanding. For example, students might add two numbers by first representing the problem by building ten-sticks out of linking cubes and then discussing what happens when the remaining ones of each addend are joined together, creating a new ten-stick. These students have the opportunity to not simply memorize addition facts but to explore what

Research Note **Focusing on Big Ideas.** Research by Jo Boaler has highlighted the many benefits of collaborative mathematics classrooms that focus on the big ideas of mathematics. In a study that compared a traditional mathematics program to a collaborative one, Boaler and Staples (2008) found that a focus on both collaboration and big ideas fostered students' understanding and enjoyment of mathematics. Further, this approach increased mathematics achievement. In more recent work, Boaler has found that a focus on big ideas supports mathematical exploration and dialogue (see the Mindset Mathematics series [Boaler, Munson, and Williams 2017–2022] and www.youcubed.org for resources).

place value is by constructing tens out of ones and reasoning about what it means to join two quantities through the mathematical act of addition. Students are able to *see* addition, investigate quantity, and make sense of place value.

6. Mathematical tasks invite and value multiple voices, conceptions, and strategies.

Because a collaborative mathematics classroom is based on exploration and dialogue, it matters that multiple ideas are at play. Simple, procedural questions meant to practice a single traditional algorithm provide little to discuss beyond how to do the procedure. Open tasks in a collaborative classroom enable discussion of multiple strategies. For example, even a simple addition expression like 32 + 67 can invite multiple ideas when students are encouraged to solve it in whatever way makes sense to them. One student might share that they imagined the problem as 30 + 60 and then 2 + 7, while another student might say that they imagined the problem as 32 + 70 and then removed the extra 3. Sharing why their strategies make sense and lead to the same answer provides rich opportunities for students to dig more deeply into numbers and also allows them to experience themselves, and others, as mathematical thinkers, learners, and community members.

> **Research Note Exploratory Tasks.** In research from the QUASAR project from the University of Pittsburgh (see *Implementing Standards-Based Mathematics Instruction: A Casebook for Professional Development* by Stein et al. 2009), researchers found that tasks that were explorative and nonalgorithmic in nature, as well as tasks that required students to make connections between mathematical ideas, were most effective at supporting learning. See *Five Practices for Orchestrating Productive Mathematical Discussion* by Smith and Stein (2011), for support in how to implement tasks that support whole-class mathematical discussions.

7. The physical environment is designed to serve students and their work with one another and mathematics.

A collaborative mathematics classroom is active, hands-on, and student led. The physical environment must be conducive to collaboration, exploration, and even a bit of a break when needed. This means that students need table arrangements that facilitate conversation and pathways around the classroom that allow them to get up, choose needed materials, and find spaces in the room where they can investigate their ideas. A collaborative classroom can get somewhat noisy and students, especially those sensitive to stimulation, may also need a quiet corner to take a moment to think on their own before rejoining their group.

Sharing Authority in a Collaborative Mathematics Classroom

In the introduction, we highlighted the centrality of shared authority in collaborative classrooms. What does that mean? Certainly the teacher remains ultimately in the driver's seat for many important reasons, but, in classrooms that share authority, aspects of the thinking work, as well as making decisions about how to work as a team, become shared between the teacher and students and among students themselves. In this section, we clarify the forms of authority that teachers must continue to hold and the specific ways they share authority with students.

Teachers' Authority

Teachers still ultimately choose what topics students will focus on, what tasks they will engage in, and what products will be turned in and assessed, as well as set expectations for work and the culture of the classroom. But by sharing authority with students, teachers shift their roles in a few important ways. They shift from being "tellers" to being *facilitators* of productive thinking and *orchestrators* of discussions by eliciting and probing students' ideas. Teachers also shift from disciplinarians to community builders, creating classroom routines with and for students that support smooth and productive collaboration and supporting student-to-student communication through a variety of resources, such as language stems or strategies for conflict resolution.

Students' Authority

Research shows us that humans learn best by constructing ideas and understandings actively, through investigations, discussions, reflections, and other aspects of inquiry. We learn best with many opportunities to make decisions, follow our curiosity, and try out possible solution paths that make sense to us. Such forms of learning not only lead to deeper understandings, but are also empowering, leading students to becoming self-directed learners invested in understanding. Students need the agency to make sense of mathematics and to engage in tasks in ways that make sense to them, developing greater capacities and understandings and more sophisticated choices. Students also need intellectual authority: the opportunity to author ideas, evaluate the ideas of others, and determine whether particular ideas make sense and are reasonable.

Interactions Are the Building Blocks of Collaboration

Classroom dynamics that empower learners arise from particular kinds of interactions that foster productive, robust, and inclusive collaboration. Research on social interactions in mathematics classrooms highlights the importance of interactions that foster (1) mathematical investigations and explorations, (2) student-led dialogue and discussion about the big ideas in mathematics, (3) respectful disagreement among students and ways to resolve issues that arise with methods that are grounded in mathematical principles, and (4) mutual recognition and regard among students as mathematical thinkers, learners, and community members.

Three strands of interactions structure this book: interactions with the environment, interactions with others, and interactions with mathematics. We will bring in research to ground this vision, highlighting connections to studies on authority, collaboration, and interaction in elementary mathematics classrooms.

Interactions with the Environment

Interactions with the environment make up the physical elements of collaboration. These include how students are oriented toward one another through the arrangement of desks, tables, and open spaces. Interactions with the environment also include how students navigate in the classroom, choosing and reaching work spaces and available resources such as manipulatives and other tools. The goal is an environment that allows for easy navigation, organization, and collaboration. Even young children should be able to walk over to a resource table, easily choose among a range of resources, and put materials away in an organized fashion. Seating arrangements should facilitate sharing resources and attending to one another's talk. (For example, round tables support eye gaze, body orientation, and side-by-side interactions that promote fairly sharing and using resources while discussing ideas with one another.)

Both classroom environments featured in "Notes from the Classroom" supported collaboration in a variety of ways. In both classrooms, the carpet served as a gathering space for reflection and practice. Faith modeled important interactions in a fishbowl, while her first graders practiced with one another before going off to interact in such ways on their own. The carpet also served as a transition space between coming back inside from an outdoor

Faith's Classroom
Environment

activity and moving into the mathematics block of the day. In Mary's classroom, space was used flexibly, as students chose where to work, creating work-
spaces out of tables or even the floor in the corner of the room. How students
interacted within the classroom environment in part shaped what was possible
for their mathematical work.

Interactions with Others

In a collaborative classroom, students regularly interact with one another. They
explain their thinking, ask one another questions, and make a variety of joint
decisions. They seek and offer attention, listen to one another, share resources,
and resolve conflicts as they arise. In doing so, they not only make sense of
mathematics together, but also develop important relationships and learn to
act as a community. Students experience themselves and one another as legitimate thinkers, learners, and community members. Teachers can introduce,
model, and practice with students particular kinds of interactions that support
joint attention, shared meaning making, and mutual recognition.

In Faith's classroom, the teacher and students discussed the questions "What does it look like when we're collaborating?" and "What does it sound like?" Faith also offered and pointed to a classroom anchor chart and other visuals to support collaborative interactions. Faith also used a fishbowl approach to model interactions, inviting Jimena and Eva to model the work of choosing a good spot to work, gathering tools and materials for the game, and negotiating who goes first. As they did so, Faith named their actions aloud to support peers' noticing of the moves they were making as collaborators and mathematicians. Whether through modeling and practicing valued interactions in preparation for a particular activity or engaged in reflective discussions about their own partnerships, students learned to interact with intentionality and in ways that fostered productive, mutual engagement in deep mathematical thinking.

Interactions with Mathematics

Of course, at the heart of a collaborative mathematics classroom is interaction with mathematical ideas. Working with one another in a conducive environment, students confront, explore, and investigate big mathematical ideas, building conceptual understanding, investigating strategies for solving problems, and considering how to mathematize their world. These learning experiences lay a strong foundation for more advanced mathematics in the later years and allow students to develop procedural fluency with understanding. Students also have the opportunity to come to understand mathematics and develop a deeper appreciation for mathematics' elegance, beauty, and power.

As we saw in Mary's description, she noted that, in her classroom, at times students came up with and implemented possible solution paths together, and other times they each tried their own ideas and then shared their thinking to come to consensus, challenge one another, or deepen their own understanding. This is rich, conceptual work laden with learning opportunities that allow students both to *understand* mathematics and experience themselves and one another as mathematical thinkers, learners, and community members.

Progression of Goals: Building a Collaborative Classroom over Time

Moving toward this vision is ongoing work. In the next four chapters, we offer goals and strategies for this work in four phases: before the school year (or, more generally, before you launch this work in your classroom, which may begin later than the start of the school year), establishing a collaborative structure, building and sharing authority, and becoming a student-led mathematics community.

We invite you to join us on this exciting journey to create active, robust collaborative classroom communities. Let's get started!

Progression of Goals for Fostering a Collaborative Math Classroom

BEFORE THE SCHOOL YEAR (Phase 1)
Chapter 2 offers guidance on how to develop and address goals for planning before you begin to introduce collaborative structures into your classroom.

ESTABLISHING A COLLABORATIVE STRUCTURE (Phase 2)
Chapter 3 addresses goals for how to begin the work with your students and establish collaborative structures from the start.

BUILDING AND SHARING AUTHORITY (Phase 3)
Chapter 4 continues the work into the school year, focused on goals for building and sharing authority between teacher and students and among students.

BECOMING A STUDENT-LED MATHEMATICS COMMUNITY (Phase 4)
Chapter 5 builds on the work from Chapter 4, deepening and expanding classroom social interactions toward becoming a student-led mathematics community.

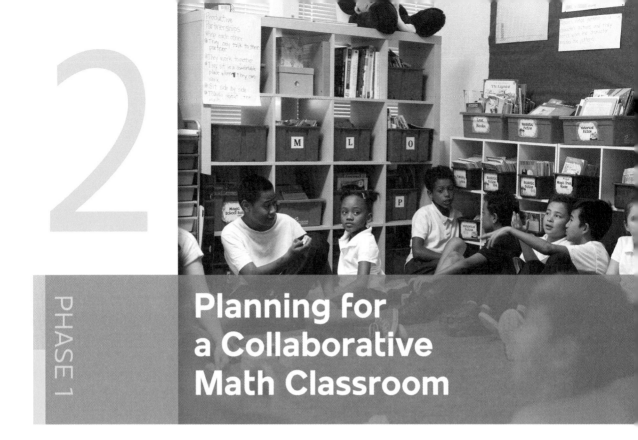

2

Planning for a Collaborative Math Classroom

Notes from the Classroom

FAITH: A Vision and Plan for Our Classroom Space

During the few teacher work days I got to set up my classroom before the school year began, I surveyed the room and wondered how I might arrange the furniture and materials so that each student felt safe and emboldened to make their own choices, each thing was accessible and had its own place, and we could all move around and through the space with ease. I started with the larger furniture pieces/areas: the rug we gather on, the six four-top tables and chairs, two low two-top tables, the kidney-shaped table for meeting with small groups, our classroom library, and a few shelves for materials and supplies. This initial setup was a draft, and as we learned about each other and spent time together in the space, revisions would happen and things would change.

With my goals in mind, I arranged the furniture, making sure to create clear pathways for walking (see Figure 2.1). I set down the rug, and thought, yes, this is a place for our meetings and lessons, but it will also be a place where students will want to lie down and read or sit cozily with partners and play games. Pillows and cushions would make it even more comfortable, but I left those in the closet by the sink, so that I could introduce them into the space intentionally later.

I turned my attention toward the shelves. They were low, so that whatever is in them would be immediately and easily accessible for six- and seven-year-olds. Although I have collected various math manipulatives over the years—teddy bear counters, rekenreks, linking cubes, clocks, 2D shapes, coins—I won't begin the year with everything on the shelves. I knew the few manipulatives the students were introduced to and used in kindergarten, and those are the bins I set out (labeled and with a picture so they remember where each thing lives).

As I closed up my classroom on the eve of the first day of school, the sight of it was calming. There was a coziness and a brightness, but a bit of a sparseness too. But this was very temporary and, starting the next day, all twenty-five of us would begin the work of making the space ours.

FIGURE 2.1
Faith's Classroom
Floor Plan

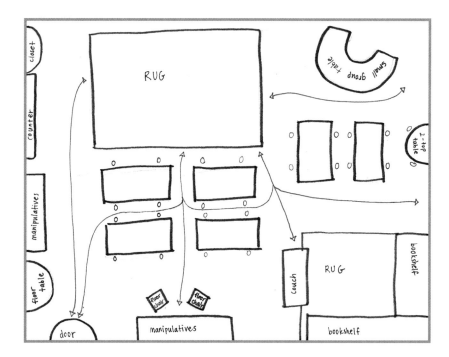

MARY: Choosing the Content for the First Math Unit

When I thought about choosing the first math unit, I had a lot to consider. I knew that my students were going to need support with building confidence, understanding what success in mathematics looks like, and learning how to work together. This complex work would be happening while my students were getting to know me and each other. My plan needed to focus on small, achievable goals that students could slowly work on—for learning mathematical concepts, developing as collaborators, and seeing themselves as mathematicians. To boost their confidence, I needed to be thoughtful about what mathematical concepts to start with. I saw two options. I could choose a unit based on number sense that would support students in building the conceptual understanding of numbers they would need for addition, subtraction, multiplication, and division. Or I could choose a unit that might trigger fewer negative memories of math learning and be more supportive of building their mathematical identities, such as geometry, measurement, or data. I ultimately decided on an addition and subtraction unit that was based on building students' understanding of the base ten system, because I felt confident that if we took the time before launching the content of the unit to explore their math identities, students would be able to be successful and have more conceptual understanding of numbers to carry them throughout the year.

E ven before the school year begins, teachers are deep in planning. We think through how to set up our classrooms. We think about how we will build relationships with students and create a community. Setting up a collaborative mathematics classroom begins with this same intentional planning. As Faith did, we think about how our students will move about the room and where and how they can work collaboratively. We also consider how rich mathematical collaboration might look and sound in our rooms. We consider the age of our students, their prior experiences with collaboration, and the particular mathematical concepts they will grapple with this year.

Like Mary, we consider what we know about the learners coming to our room and decide what unit to start the year with. We choose activities and tasks that will support collecting formative assessment data about students' understanding of collaboration and mathematics. This planning phase helps us be thoughtful and creative about how we see our students learning and proactively prepare to bring this vision to life.

In this chapter, we will share goals for planning for a collaborative mathematics classroom, from setting up the classroom space to envisioning how students could work together to choosing mathematical work for the beginning of the year. We describe what each goal means and provide reflective questions for you to consider as you plan. We also describe three planning strategies that can support you as you prepare to launch your collaborative mathematics classroom.

Goals for Planning for a Collaborative Math Classroom

The goals for interactions with the environment, others, and mathematics in this phase focus on planning, setting up the classroom space, imagining how students will work and move, choosing a mathematical unit, and anticipating what students will need (see Figure 2.2). In the sections that follow, we examine each of the six goals in more detail.

Goals for Interactions With . . .			
	Environment	**Others**	**Mathematics**
PHASE 1 **Planning for a Collaborative Math Classroom**	• Set up the classroom space so that students can access materials and resources without the support of the teacher. • Arrange furniture to support students to engage in joint work and to move freely. • Set up the classroom with multiple potential math work spaces.	• Consider what productive collaborations could look like for your students.	• Select a first few days' activities that allow students to begin to engage in collaborative work and you to assess their interactions and mathematics knowledge. • Select a first unit that will allow students to do some meaningful mathematics but focus more on building interactions.

FIGURE 2.2 Goals for Phase 1: Planning a Collaborative Math Classroom

Interactions with the Environment

When planning for the new school year, the physical environment is often at the front of teachers' minds. It is a time to reset, reflect on the ways the classroom has worked and could work better, and try new configurations of furniture and materials. It is no wonder then that three of our goals in this planning phase center on preparing the physical environment to support collaboration. The physical environment sends messages to students about their roles, authority, and expectations, by making some spaces and materials readily available and others more peripheral. To ensure that your environment supports your aims of developing a collaborative math classroom, you will want to keep the following goals in mind:

- Set up the classroom space so that students can access materials and resources without the support of the teacher.
- Arrange furniture to support students to engage in joint work and to move freely.
- Set up the classroom with multiple potential math work spaces.

Set up the classroom space so that students can access materials and resources without the support of the teacher.

Mathematics requires tools for representing and modeling, from snap cubes, base ten blocks, and rekenreks representing tens and ones, to grid paper, square tiles, and objects in bowls representing arrays or equal groups. For students to work together to make sense of mathematics, they need the authority to choose how to model mathematical situations. This is inherently part of the mathematical practices of developing solution pathways and modeling with mathematics. Students need access to the necessary resources and the authority to choose and gather the materials that make sense to them in the moment. Appropriate manipulatives and tools should be stored within easy sight and reach of students, so that they can get up from their work space and retrieve what they need as they work.

To plan your space for access to materials and resources, think about the following questions:

- What manipulatives will you introduce early in the year? Which will you wait to introduce? What have your students already had experience with? These decisions connect back to the first unit you will teach, which we will discuss a little later in the chapter.

Mary's Classroom
Environment

- What choices will you make available? Don't overwhelm students with too many choices and materials they have never seen. Think about simple tools that are flexible and powerful, such as snap cubes, square tiles, and grid or chart paper, along with those that are particularly important in your first unit.
- Where will you store materials for ready access? Are there any supplies that you expect to use every day (such as grid paper, cubes, or base ten blocks) that you want located where students work, like on tables? Where could you store communal materials? Shelves or counters?
- How can you make access easy and intuitive? Students need to be able to find, retrieve, and return materials. Consider how to use labels (with words and/or pictures) or cluster supplies into one space so that students know where to go when they need a tool for math.

In the end, you'll want to choose a set of materials to make readily available at the beginning of the year, along with an organizational structure that you can grow and adapt as you move into new units of study and students build familiarity with a wider selection of tools. For instance, Mary began the year with two materials important to the first unit she selected: base ten blocks and linking cubes. She set up a shelf with multiple bins of each of these tools, and students from each table could retrieve a set, as needed. These same shelves could later hold new manipulatives (such as geoboards and pattern blocks) as the class transitioned into new math units.

Arrange furniture to support students to engage in joint work and move freely.

Collaboration is a physical act that requires space. How students and materials are arranged in relation to one another affects how they can work together. Collaborating students need to be able to see, touch, and share written work and manipulatives. They need to be able to move freely to find appropriate spaces to work, show one another their thinking, and access tools.

Often we don't have choices about the furniture available for our classrooms. If you do, choose items that don't crowd the space and are flexible enough to support many different kinds of collaboration. Tables, for instance, are much more flexible than individual desks, which tend to constrain the space available to the group. If, like most teachers, you are limited to the furniture you have on hand, then the most important choices you can make are how to arrange it for movement and discussion.

To plan your space for collaboration and movement, consider the following questions:

- How can you arrange furniture to enable partners to sit side by side or groups to face one another? For groups to collaborate, there needs to be a clear joint working space that everyone can see and reach.
- Are the surfaces large enough to accommodate both materials and shared written work?
- How can you make spaces wide enough to allow for free movement? How can you avoid bottlenecks in traffic flow? Consider, also, where materials will be stored and how students will need to move through the room to access them.
- When it is time for discussion, where will students gather to share and see one another's thinking? Collaboration does not require that students always face the same way as they work. But when it is time

to discuss students' mathematical ideas, they will need to be able to see each other and any representations of those ideas. Many teachers address this with a rug or other common gathering space separate from students' work space.

Perhaps counterintuitively, less furniture is often more flexible, creating more room to move and work. Consider starting the year with a leaner classroom that you can add to if needed.

Set up the classroom with multiple potential math work spaces.

While group tables are certainly the most commonly used shared work space for collaboration, they are only one possibility. Students may prefer to work on the floor, on the classroom rug, at extra tables, in the hallway, or in nooks or corners. Some students might become overwhelmed by the activity of a collaborating classroom and want to move with a partner to a more sheltered space. And sometimes the mathematical work itself demands a larger venue for assembling large quantities of blocks or recording thinking on a piece of chart paper. Students work together in a variety of ways and need the authority to choose a quieter, more private, larger, or more relaxed space to work, depending on their needs.

Your role at this point in the year is to create spaces that students might choose from to meet these needs. These spaces do not need to be large, just varied and available by choice. For instance, we know teachers who have turned an old coat closet with the doors removed into a quieter partner work space. Others have converted an unused corner into a work zone with a pair of beanbag chairs or cushions. Classroom libraries can be math spaces, as can kidney tables used for guided reading. You'll want spaces where students can spread out for big work with lots of materials, small spaces for partners, and quieter spaces for those who need less stimulation. See Figure 2.3 for an example of a first-draft floor plan that considers how students might collaborate in multiple spaces and move around the room.

As you map out the possible work spaces, consider the following questions:

- What spaces can you create and offer to students to choose to work in together?
- How can you make these spaces functional for math work? Students might benefit from cushions or carpet squares for comfort. They may need access to clipboards for writing or containers for carrying tools.

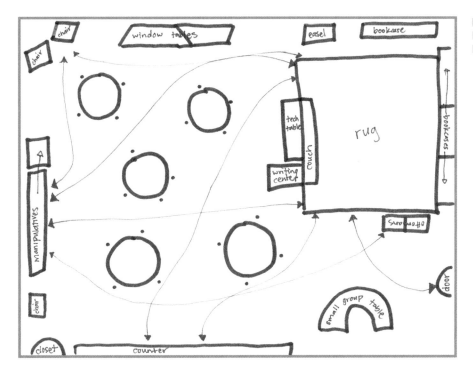

FIGURE 2.3
Mary's Classroom
Floor Plan

- What will the norms be for working in these spaces? These norms will need to be set with the class. For instance, you may need to indicate how many students can fit in each space or what pathways can and cannot be blocked.

- How should students decide who gets to use which space if there are conflicts? Are there particular uses that get priority? Students will undoubtedly want to work in the same spaces, and this can generate conflict. Some students may need the space, and others may only want it. For instance, some students may struggle to focus sitting upright at a table and may be better able to engage in math thinking sprawled on the rug, and other students may simply want the comfort of the carpet. Consider how you want students to decide who gets a space if more than one group wants to claim it. Will there be a rotation? Should students use rock-paper-scissors? Will you adjudicate?

Creating multiple, flexible math collaboration spaces should also make your classroom more flexible during all parts of the day. By the same token, if you have made flexible spaces for, say, reading, you can make use of them in mathematics, too.

Interactions with Others

Though of course students' interactions with others will not begin until they are in your classroom, your planning time is a prime opportunity to envision how you want those interactions to unfold, given the experiences you expect students will have already had with mathematical collaboration. Because this is anticipatory work, we have just one, juicy goal for you to keep in mind:

- Consider what productive collaborations could look like for your students.

BUILDING A VISION OF COLLABORATION

MARY

I will know my students are collaborating when I see them depending on each other rather than needing my approval or support. This looks like students looking at their partner's work and pointing, looking at each other when they are having a math-related conversation, moving about the room with ease, and getting more materials or reading anchor charts. The noise level in the room fluctuates with bursts of excitement or disagreement. But the biggest sign is that students are talking about math with one another using their own words. When this happens, I know they are truly working together, valuing each other's ideas, and listening to learn.

FAITH

I will know my students are collaborating when I notice a shared direction, an agreed-upon next step. This is not always an immediate and efficient start on the task. Sometimes this looks like playing rock-paper-scissors to decide who goes first or stacking linking cubes in rods of ten, helping each other find and alternate their favorite colors (not necessary for the task at hand, but important to them nonetheless). Sometimes this sounds like a question or suggestion, starting with "Maybe we can . . ." or "What if we . . ." as they figure out a good place to work or sit down, and one student realizes they don't have the materials they need. The volume is always variable, as is movement around the room, but there is an easiness and intention at the heart of it all. I know they are collaborating when I can approach a student at an anchor chart, or a partnership walking toward a shelf, and ask how it's going, and they share a plan or an immediate next step or the question they are talking through.

Consider what productive collaborations could look like for your students.

Although this goal may sound like a mere exercise, carefully imaging students collaborating with one another in your classroom is a key step toward creating that classroom. In fact, you can't plan for what you can't envision. There is no one-size-fits-all approach; imagining your particular students collaborating can help you prepare to teach them to do so and plan the environment and mathematical work that will support them.

Try the following thought experiment. Write a story of how you imagine your students collaborating midyear. Picture a particular lesson or moment. What does the collaboration look and sound like? Try storyboarding what you might see and hear in your imagined classroom. (See more about storyboarding on page 29.) Consider these questions:

- Are you imagining pairs or small groups?
- How and where are the students grouped? What does their body language look like?
- What kinds of work might they collaborate on: problem-solving, games, projects?
- How often do you imagine students collaborating? Every day? Less?
- What would it sound like as you circulate around the room? What words might you overhear as you circulate?
- How long would you like your students at their developmental stage to be able to sustain collaboration without your intervention?

Some of this envisioning work might change your thinking about your physical environment. Revision is a sign of growth!

As you envision your collaborative classroom, you can begin to ask yourself, "What will students need to learn to do to collaborate this way?" For instance, it may not be obvious to all students that they will need to put materials in a place where both they and their partners can see, reach, and share them. But if students huddled around a shared paper or collection of manipulatives is part of your vision, you and they will be more successful if you teach them how to do just that. You might start a list of what collaboration looks and sounds like that could eventually become a list of learning goals for your class.

Interactions with Mathematics

Before the school year begins, you will need to map out the mathematical work you plan to engage students in during the first week and month of school. The mathematical work you choose sends powerful messages about what it means to do mathematics, who can do mathematics, and how doing mathematics will look for the remainder of the year. These first weeks also help you build capacity for students to do the very kind of collaborative work you envisioned. As you plan for the coming school year, you will want to keep the following goals in mind:

- Select a first few days' activities that allow students to begin to engage in collaborative work and you to assess their interactions and mathematics knowledge.
- Select a first unit that will allow students to do some meaningful mathematics but focus more on building interactions.

Select the first few days' activities that allow students to begin to engage in collaborative work and you to assess their interactions and mathematics knowledge.

In the first few days of school, students are getting acclimated to the ways that your classroom works and to one another. During this time, you'll want to engage them in some initial mathematical tasks that have two features:

1. **Openness:** Choose open tasks that involve mathematical thinking, ones in which the floor is low enough for all to enter, and that can be solved in numerous possible ways. This will allow you to do a lot of observing and not spend as much time helping students understand or enter the task. Open tasks also communicate to students that mathematics itself is open to multiple ways of thinking, doing, and knowing.
2. **Formative assessment:** Choose tasks that allow you to assess students' prior knowledge and their processes for making sense of the content. You might select content from the previous year that will immediately influence how they engage in the first unit or the whole year. You can observe how students engage in mathematical practices such as perseverance, finding a solution pathway, modeling, attending to structure, or justification.

One of the initial tasks might include exploration of math materials, such as snap cubes, base ten blocks, pattern blocks, coins, or square tiles. You might simply invite students to explore what they can do with these tools or what they can represent. Such exploration time helps students build familiarity with tools they will need in the early units of the year and creates space for playfulness. (This relates to one of the goals for the next phase, which we will discuss in Chapter 3.) Some additional examples of open tasks that create opportunities for formative assessment include:

- Come up with as many ways as you can to represent 34. Use this task to assess how students handle an open task, negotiate with a partner, model with mathematics, and understand place value.
- Show students an image from the real world and ask, "What do you notice? What do you wonder?" You can launch this task as a whole group and then provide students with printed copies of the image to discuss and annotate with a partner. See examples of this type of activity at multiplicitylab.northwestern.edu.
- Provide students with manipulatives, such as snap cubes, dominoes, coins, or pattern blocks, and ask, "What patterns can you make? How could you describe your patterns?" Use this task to assess students' understanding of patterning and structure and how they interact with others to show and describe patterns.
- Pose a problem that has multiple solutions: "I have some coins and you have some coins. Together we have 50 cents. What coins might we each have?" Use this to assess how students handle a task with multiple answers, decomposing numbers, place value, skip counting, thinking in fives and tens, and organizing for solving repeatedly.
- Provide partners with a collection of objects, such as buttons, beads, or small toys, and ask, "How could you organize these objects?" Use this to assess how students share resources with a partner, attend to attributes, and create structure.

Choose activities that will allow you to observe how students interact with mathematical ideas and practices and with one another.

In addition to these full-lesson activities, Mary and Faith both start the year with dot talks, in which students are shown an arrangement of dots and asked, "How many do you see? How do you see them?" (Parrish 2010). Dot talks, regardless of your grade level, offer a key place to establish routines and norms around mathematical discussion, the value of multiple strategies, and the nature of math as open and creative. As an upper-elementary grade teacher, Mary also finds that taking away the stigma of numbers also allows her students to understand that learners see math differently and that this is something valued in her community. This routine also helps to add curiosity and wonder to math.

Select a first unit that will allow students to do some meaningful mathematics but focus more on building interactions.

The first unit of instruction should invite students into participation. That means that students should feel that they have access to the mathematical ideas and can be successful. This unit sets the tone for the ways you want students to do math for the whole year. In some schools, the units of instruction are chosen for you, but if you have a choice, there are a number of factors to consider. In a first unit, you want:

- a focus on big mathematical ideas (rather than individual standards, procedures, or vocabulary), where those ideas build on and extend learning from previous grades and open the door to concepts and materials you will use throughout the year
- open tasks that can be solved in multiple ways
- tasks that benefit from discourse and collaboration, where there is something juicy to talk about
- opportunities for students who have previously not experienced success in math to find ways to participate and enjoy mathematics

These criteria might mean that you want to start with a unit focused on number in some way, because ideas about number have been built across years and will support students throughout the school year. Faith, for instance, starts the year with a number unit with a concept from kindergarten: making ten. By giving students something that's mathematically familiar, they can focus their attention on learning how to attend to each other's thinking. Mary similarly begins the year with a number unit, one with a focus on addition and subtraction, a topic that students are revisiting from previous years. What is new for students is the way they are being asked to do mathematics. She uses a unit developed by Cathy Fosnot (2008) that is rich enough that students are going to be able to explore familiar mathematics through inquiry and be challenged. Or you might opt to choose a unit where number is not front and center, such

Research Note The Cognitive Demand of Math Tasks. A great task involves thinking and figuring out, not regurgitating known information or performing rote procedures. In analyzing mathematical tasks, Stein and Smith (1998) created a four-level framework for categorizing the kind of mathematical work asked of students, or their *cognitive demand*. The four levels include two with lower-level cognitive demand—(1) memorization and (2) procedures without connections—and two with higher-level cognitive demand—(3) procedures with connections and (4) doing mathematics. Using tasks categorized as *doing mathematics* is our goal as math teachers, because these ask students to do "complex and non-algorithmic thinking" (p. 348), demand exploration and understanding of concepts, and require students to struggle. These tasks do not fit a blueprint with a clear solution pathway; part of their challenge is that students must carve out a pathway themselves, often making mistakes and trying new ideas along the way. Such tasks are ideally suited to collaboration because different students can contribute different forms of knowledge, pose different kinds of questions, and generate different ideas, all of which might move the group forward toward finding a solution.

as geometry, measurement, or data, because these strands of mathematics can welcome students who are often excluded from feeling successful in math. In the appendix, we have included a list of resources for units of instruction that we think provide meaningful tasks for all students as a reference.

If you do not get to choose what unit to teach first, then consider the previous list as a tool for choosing resources or modifying the resources you do have. You can make tasks more open, shift the focus from a procedure to deeper understanding, or remove some of the structures (like worksheets) that constrain what is possible for problem-solving.

Planning to Launch the Year

With these goals in mind, here are three planning tools that may help you as you plan to launch the school year. Making a floor plan can support you in planning your physical environment. Storyboarding student collaboration can help you develop your vision for what collaboration might look and sound like in your math classroom. Consulting with your curricular resources can support you in making decisions about tasks and units.

Make a Floor Plan

Floor plans allow you to dream up new ways of arranging your physical environment, move furniture around, and get creative, without doing the heavy lifting until you are ready. You can make a floor plan by hand with grid paper or using digital tools. Start by measuring your room and furniture. Find out what options you have for furniture; it may be that there are pieces you can swap out if you ask. Make individual movable components (digitally or on paper) for each piece of furniture proportional to the room size. Then start to lay out furniture in different ways. Locate the different kinds of spaces you'll need, such as a gathering space, private work areas, collaboration spaces, and various kinds of storage. Consider where materials will be kept, both in what pieces of furniture and where that furniture will go in relation to where students will likely work. Think about traffic flow: How will students move through the space to get to work areas, gathering spaces, and materials? Try to avoid bottlenecks or narrow walkways that will congest movement or lead to some students constantly getting their chairs bumped by others passing by. Check your plan against your goals. What works about this arrangement? What is still not entirely satisfactory? Take a picture of your arrangement, and then try again:

What else is possible? Pressing yourself to come up with new solutions can foster creativity and ideas you might not have thought of.

Storyboard Collaboration for Students in Your Grade Level

Envisioning how students in your grade and in your class might collaborate requires disciplined imagination. To plan and teach, you must move beyond generalities and think concretely about what collaboration in your classroom could look and sound like. We suggest storyboarding as a tool to press yourself to get specific about this vision. With a colleague or on your own, try to imagine exactly what it could look like or sound like for two or more students in your school and grade level to work together on a task. Use the following guiding questions to help you:

- What are students saying to each other?
- What would it sound like if they were building on each other's ideas and taking each other seriously?
- What space, materials, and words would they need?
- How are students' bodies positioned, in the room and in relation to one another?
- Where are their materials, such as paper and manipulatives?

To get even more concrete, imagine your students are working on one of the following tasks. What would you hope you would see and hear?

- I have a box of 10 apples. Some are red and some are green. How many red apples might be in the box? How many green apples might be in the box? Find as many ways as you can to fill the box. (Adapted from Fosnot 2008)
- What numbers can you make with 12 base ten blocks? How will you know when you've found all the possibilities? (Adapted from Boaler, Munson, and Williams 2022)
- I made a pattern out of yellow and blue square tiles. I used twice as many blue tiles as yellow tiles. What might the pattern have looked like?

As you imagine what students look and sound like, sketch out what you see, either in a single snapshot picture or a series of images like a graphic novel. There is no need to be an artist; you can capture quite a lot with stick figures. Then, talk your storyboard over with a colleague. Your colleague may have other ideas that build on yours or may have their own storyboard to share with you. Consider what students will need to learn to move toward your vision. We know they are not there yet, and naming what they need will help you imagine teaching them how to get there.

Consult Your Curricular Resources

Most teachers have curricular resources for teaching mathematics in the form of texts, units, tasks, games, or calendars. As you begin to plan for the mathematical work that students might do in the first days, weeks, and unit, these resources can be pivotal to your decision making. Begin by asking the following questions:

- What control do you have over the following areas?
  - ▶ How much can you vary or select elements of your curriculum?
  - ▶ Can you add, skip, or modify tasks?
  - ▶ Can you modify or select forms of assessment?
  - ▶ To what degree can you determine the sequence of units?

- What resources do you have to draw on?
  - ▶ What curriculum resources are available? (See the appendix for recommended resources.)
  - ▶ What mathematics standards are you responsible for teaching toward?
  - ▶ What other professional tools (such as professional texts, professional development, or videos) might you access?
  - ▶ What colleagues (including fellow teachers, coaches, and specialists) could you tap as thought partners?

Even when curriculum is provided and schedules are decided, you likely can choose to modify tasks to make them more open and worthy of collaboration. For instance, some of the richest mathematical work is often buried near the end of lessons as extensions or enrichment. Many games that are used for practice could instead be modified to be genuine exploration if done early in the unit rather than at the end. Many tasks are written to have one right answer but could be modified to be open to many possible answers. Look at your resources and ask, "Where are the best lessons, activities, and tasks? Which lessons, activities, or tasks could become richer by making a few modifications?" (See the appendix for recommended resources on modifying tasks.)

We also encourage you to rethink taken-for-granted decisions about curriculum. Just because something has always been done one way does not mean you need to continue that way. For instance, do you always begin the year with Unit One of a textbook because you have to, or simply out of inertia? Is there a different unit that might get students engaged and better promote collaboration? Use your resources to determine what choices you do have, and then make the decisions that best promote the kind of mathematical community you hope to foster.

Questions to Consider as You Plan to Launch Your Year

Here are a few questions you might think through as you pursue the goals of this phase with your specific students and in your context:

- How do you want your students to feel in the classroom?
- What do you want students to be able to do for themselves?
- What choices about where and how to work do you want students to have?
- What big ideas in mathematics are you focusing on this year?
- What big ideas do you want students to engage with at the beginning of the year? Which big ideas will most students find accessible and engaging?
- What do you already know about your students or their prior experiences in mathematics?
- What open-ended tasks do you have access to? Where in your curriculum or resources can you find these?
- What colleagues do you have that might share your vision for collaboration? How could you plan or work together this year?

If . . . Then . . .

In this section we offer some thoughts on common situations that arise during this phase of planning for a collaborative math classroom.

If you are planning to launch a collaborative math classroom midyear, then . . .

Shifting the way you teach and students learn math midyear is entirely possible, but it does pose some challenges you'll want to plan for. First, you have already established a classroom environment and routines for working that will need some revision. Reflect on each of these and ponder, "What parts of my current classroom environment/math routines are supporting my vision of a collaborative math classroom? Which parts of my current classroom environment/math routines would I like to revise to better support collaboration?" Make a detailed list of the aspects you'd like to change and how. Remember that the physical environment will be the easiest to change, whereas changes in ways students interact with one another will take time to take root. Plan a launch date that takes advantage of a natural transition, such as a change of unit or returning from a school break.

Talk to your students in advance about the changes you are planning to make and, most importantly, *why*. Talk with your students about your vision of your collaborative math classroom and how you believe it will support their thinking and learning. Bring them on board as partners in this experiment and acknowledge that there may be bumps along the way. These kinds of honest, open conversations accomplish several goals. First, they reinforce the intent of collaboration by bringing students into collaboration with you on this new work together. Second, they allow students to make sense of the changes they will experience and the rationale behind them. Third, they lower the stakes on your efforts by acknowledging this is a process, and revision and mistakes are normal.

If you are at a new school and have little background information on your students, then . . .

Use this as an opportunity to meet your colleagues and get to know the school culture. Ask to chat with the previous grade-level teachers and ask some general questions about your students' math experiences during the prior year, such as "What did math time look like last year? How did students work together? How did students share their ideas with one another? Did they ever do any group work or group projects? How did that look?" Your goal is just to glean some background information about their experiences that can help you understand what might be new or familiar territory for them.

If, on the other hand, you have students you cannot learn about this way (for instance, because you teach kindergarten or have many students new to your school), you'll need to include in your plans for the beginning of the year lots of opportunities to observe students at work. Watching students work (and play) together is still the most valuable way to gather data on what they know how to do. Consider planning more days for initial exploration of materials to see how students naturally interact, work together, or build on one another's observations or ideas.

If your students have had a lot of prior experience with math collaboration, then . . .

Celebrate! Consider talking to the previous years' teachers to find out about the norms and routines they used. Once you know more about what students have experienced before, you can decide which of these norms or routines you want to keep or build on. For instance, if the previous grade level used a chart to show math partners and changed these at the end of each unit, you might decide to keep this structure, make your own chart, and point out to students that you will be partnering in math this year just like they did in the past. Even if you decide not to keep or build on a collaborative structure from previous years, knowing what students have experienced can allow you to help students transition. For instance, you might say, "I know that last year you used a chart to assign partners for math, but this year we're going to work on learning how to choose your own partner, one who you can be productive with."

You may also want to review our goals in the coming chapters with an eye toward assessing what students likely already know how to do, what they might need to be reminded of, what they have started learning, and what may still be new. You can adjust and adapt your plans to spend more or less time on these goals based on your assessment of their experience. However, just as with launching any new year, students need to know what *your* expectations are; remember that even with prior experience students will still need to be taught what it means to collaborate in your classroom, in the tasks you give them, and around the math ideas at your grade level.

If your students have had no prior experience with math collaboration, then . . .

Go slow, plan carefully, and focus on modest goals. Remember what it takes to bring students into anything new in your classroom. Routines and structures often differ from class to class or grade to grade, and any different way of working has to be intentionally and incrementally taught. You may want to plan to start your year by acknowledging directly that math is going to look different this year and sharing why you want to have students work together instead of alone. The more transparent you can be, the less confused children are likely to be about the shift or what is expected of them. For instance, you might plan to gather students on the carpet and ask, "What did a typical day in math look like last year?" This conversation can be a useful form of assessment for you and a bridge to saying, "This year we're going to try it differently." You can tell students that they will be learning how to work together, because learning happens when we talk about and do math together, trying to figure things out. You might plan to point out that it takes work to figure out math ideas and it takes work to figure out how to collaborate; math time will be about both of these things this year.

Finally, remember that this book was written for you. Mary and Faith each had to establish collaborative classrooms when students did not have experience collaborating in math the previous year. In creating this resource for you, we assume that your students do not have experience collaborating in mathematics.

If you have no other grade-level colleagues planning for a collaborative math classroom, then . . .

Cast a wide net for colleagues you can talk to about your goals. For instance, Faith and Mary taught in the same school but very different grades; they were not well positioned to co-plan math lessons together because the math concepts their students were learning were so different. However, they became collegial resources for one another to discuss what it means to collaborate in mathematics, the instructional strategies they had developed to foster collaboration, and issues that arose in their efforts. They found both ways in which their work differed because of the developmental stages of their students and common ground in consistent patterns, problems, and strategies across grade levels. Look all around your building for teachers trying this work in their own ways. If your school has a math coach, that person could also be your partner. If your school has math interventionists or specialists who move from class to class, they may know which teachers invite students to work together. Finally, you may need partners outside your building who can serve as thought partners; ask those you know at other school sites to help you find a colleague.

If you have a mandated curriculum, scope, and sequence, then . . .

Figure out what agency you have and use it. For instance, if the district requires that you use a curriculum with a preselected first unit, then you might still be able to choose *how* you use this resource. Even if the published lesson plan assumes you will assign individual work, you could plan for students to engage in activities with a partner. If the curriculum involves repetitive calculations, you might use just one or two of these and ask students to figure out how to solve them rather than showing them a procedure. Often curricula have richer problems, games, and activities buried at the back of lessons or units. You could decide to use these first, rather than as optional extensions, to address the same mathematical ideas. The curriculum may not call for a closing discussion or sharing methods, but you could add this to any lesson. Even with mandates, you often have the discretion to make decisions about how to implement the curriculum. Embrace your discretion and look for opportunities within the framework you've been provided to give students a chance to work together on meaningful mathematics.

Establishing a Collaborative Structure

Notes from the Classroom

FAITH: "Maybe We Can . . . I Go First?"

Before I met my first graders, I had the opportunity to observe two of my students in a math partnership as kindergarteners. They were tasked with finding different combinations of five red and green apples in a box, and they spent the entirety of their work time arguing over who got to hold the red crayon. Totally natural—and yet, here were two students who did not get the opportunity to interact with the math work because they were very busy negotiating how to share materials. I had the luxury in the moment of not being their teacher and considering how I could support them and other students in similar conflicts beyond a quick fix. Yes, I could just tell them to use rock-paper-scissors, I could get them a second red crayon, I could tell them to take turns and arbitrarily assign one of the students the first turn. Although I've done and continue to do and say all these things (with mixed results, because these are six-year-olds), I also know that when *I* solve their problem, I'm not giving *them* the opportunity to negotiate, collaborate, and internalize those skills.

To try to address this challenge back in my first-grade class, I introduced the phrase "Maybe we can . . ." within the context of partner negotiations— the idea of sharing the decision-making power with your partner rather than making a demand. We circled up and thought, then talked about how it makes us feel if our partner says, "I want the red crayon!" or "I'm going first!" That may make us feel upset, or like we don't want to work with our partner, or that it's not fair that they get to go first. I asked my students if they thought asking questions, like "Maybe we can . . . ?" instead of telling would help us collaborate better.

We decided to try it out in a fishbowl. I sat in the middle with a student partner and we acted out getting ready to work on a math task together. We created a conflict: "I want to hold the crayon!" "No, I want to hold the crayon!" I called out, "Freeze!" and had the students discuss what we might say instead, offering the phrase, "Maybe we can . . ." Some students shared their ideas, "Maybe we can . . . rock-paper-scissors?" "Maybe we can . . . take turns?" "Maybe we can . . . each hold a different crayon?" As students shared, we repeated in chorus, to practice using that phrase.

It is now October, and most launches into partner work include a quick minute-long brainstorm of "Maybe we cans" as we consider conflicts that may come up. Today I stopped to listen in on a partnership in negotiation and heard, "Maybe we can . . . I go first?" This suggestion, although not exactly what I had in mind, was met, surprisingly, with enthusiasm from her partner. She went first, and they got to work. Right now, I celebrate the approximation and make a note to continue the practice, discussion, and reflection.

MARY: Beyond the Algorithm

One day in September, I launched us into the task for the day, a subtraction problem where a boy owns a T-shirt factory: He has 176 T-shirts and sold 82. How many does he have left? I set the students up to be able to engage with the subtraction task: we read the problem together, I acted it out in front of them, and I had a student explain the story. I said, "Turn and talk about the strategy you will use today to solve the problem." I listened in on the student conversations, and I didn't hear students sharing potentially successful strategies that I could name to the group. When I called students back together I asked, "What strategies did you all come up with?" The students stared at me blankly. They did not have ideas for how to approach this task. In the moment, I had a few options. I could model a strategy of my own, I could let them go off and grapple how to solve this problem using their own strategies, or I could make up a strategy and share it as if it was a student strategy. I had a feeling that if I sent them off, they would continue to struggle with how to get started. I knew they were not yet used to having the authority to choose how to figure out a problem. I decided to let them try to solve the problem without any guidance because I didn't want them to think that I was the person responsible for telling them how to do the math. The students were used to the teacher modeling a strategy that they copied and applied to more problems. I sent them off without a strategy hoping that the productive struggle would lead students to being open to a conversation about how to approach coming up with a strategy.

While students were working, I circulated the room hoping I would see a strategy for solving subtraction problems other than the traditional algorithm that I could bring back to the whole group. I was looking for any glimmer of a picture, decomposing numbers using place value, or even a number line. I knew this was a risky move, but I wanted the students to know that I wasn't going to save them from the hard work of figuring out problems on their own. Sure enough, there were two partnerships that drew models of the story. They had drawn all the T-shirts from the problem and had begun to cross off each of the shirts that were being sold. This was not an efficient strategy by any means, but it was student invented and it was a way to show students how to model a problem based on the context. I knew this would be the strategy that I highlighted during the discussion.

I brought the students to the carpet and asked the partnerships to bring their notebook. I said, "I noticed during the launch today a lot of you were struggling to come up with a strategy. Allisson and Jacky came up with a strategy that seemed to work, so I asked them to share it with you all. Allisson and Jacky, can you show us your notebooks while you are explaining?" At this point in the year, students still struggle to explain their thinking, but I knew their example would at least give others an idea for how to start work tomorrow, even if Allisson and Jacky's explanation was not yet completely clear. This work time might have seemed like it wasn't a successful day, but my moves were intentional and with the goals of building a math community in mind. I was able to show students I trusted them to figure out the work on their own and that there isn't one right way to do math work.

Launching ways of learning mathematics together in classrooms is complex work that requires teachers to have a clear vision of their goals and to communicate their vision in ways that invite students to be codesigners. This means that sometimes students need to be shown how to do something, and other times they need to be asked instead, "How could we do this so it works for everyone?"

Right from the beginning, there are many things for students to learn that get the classroom engine humming. Students need to know how to access manipulatives and use the physical space of the classroom to accomplish mathematical work. They need to know what it means to collaborate with a partner to solve a mathematics problem, including how to talk and listen to each other, make sense of one another's mathematical strategies and ways of thinking, and recognize themselves and one another as doers and learners of mathematics. And they need to know that doing mathematics involves struggle, risk-taking, mistakes, sensemaking, connection, and creativity. As in Mary's note, this can require some uncomfortable moments of allowing students to grapple with ambiguity. Students need to learn how to manage these situations while also taking ownership of the process and exercising their voices. In this phase of establishing a collaborative structure, we have to actively dance with students, where sometimes we lead, and sometimes they do. This is a long process where challenges are opportunities to learn and each step toward collaboration deserves recognition. In this chapter, we'll focus on how to establish these foundational ways of working in the classroom right off the bat.

Research Note **Ownership = Agency + Authority.** In the math classroom, teachers hold a lot of authority (Amit and Fried 2005). Teachers explain and evaluate math ideas and decide who speaks, when, and for what reasons. In collaborative classrooms, teachers share some of this authority with students (Langer-Osuna 2018; Yackel and Cobb 1996). During whole-class discussions, students share their thinking, explain mathematical ideas, and evaluate the ideas of others. In small-group work, students also manage turn taking and roles. By sharing their ideas, responding to the ideas of others, and sharing in the management of collaborative tasks, students develop a sense of mathematical agency. To do this well, however, students must also learn how to communicate and negotiate with one another in productive and inclusive ways.

One of the key moves at the beginning of the year is to promote reflective thought and conversation with your students about what it looks like and sounds like to do mathematics together. Reflections can center on questions about what partners can do to work together, what strategies made sense and why, what was successful or challenging about a partnership, or how students used space or tools to support their thinking. Teachers also want to suggest concrete, actionable moves students can make to support productive collaboration, whether these come directly from students' own experiences or are taught by the teacher, as in Faith's example.

In this chapter, we will examine the foundational goals for beginning collaborative mathematical work with students, supporting them to use and choose math tools, make choices together, and help shape what doing mathematics in our classrooms will mean. Particularly if your students have never experienced a collaborative mathematics classroom, these changes can represent a radical shift, and this phase may take some time. We'll share examples from Mary and Faith's teaching of how they roll out these goals with their own students, so that you can consider what might work for you and your students. We'll invite you to look for signs to celebrate and discuss some common situations that develop at this stage. Along the way we'll share with you some key ideas from research that support your efforts to establish a collaborative mathematics classroom.

Goals for Establishing a Collaborative Structure

Your classroom needs a structure upon which to build the rest of the year. Laying this foundation takes time and involves teaching students how they can move and work in your classroom space, how they can interact productively with one another, and what doing mathematics means. These are the building blocks for routines and norms that structure collaboration, and as teachers, we cannot take for granted that students will learn them implicitly or know intuitively how to "work together." In this phase, we see nine key goals, three each for interacting with the environment, others, and mathematics (see Figure 3.1). In the sections that follow, we examine each of these goals, what they mean, and how you might move toward them.

Goals for Interactions With . . .		
Environment	**Others**	**Mathematics**
PHASE 2 Establishing a Collaborative Structure • Introduce the space and tools and what we use them for. • Provide structured time to explore space and tools. • Support students to choose a space to work where they can be productive.	• As a class, define what a productive partnership means. • Support students in being and choosing a productive partner. • Support students with negotiating how to get started with collaboration.	• Begin to define what doing mathematics means in this space. • Send a clear message about what constitutes mathematical success and recognize examples immediately. • Establish a clear lesson structure that includes a launch, an exploration, and a discussion.

FIGURE 3.1 Goals for Phase 2: Establishing a Collaborative Structure

Interactions with the Environment

Students need to know how to access manipulatives and other materials and use the physical space of the classroom to accomplish mathematical work. While maintaining flexibility in the ways the classroom environment can look and function, we can establish a structure that supports students in making decisions together and begins the work of authentic collaboration. We will want to keep the following goals in mind:

- Introduce the space and tools and what we use them for.
- Provide structured time to explore space and tools.
- Support students to choose a space to work where they can be productive.

Introduce the space and tools and what we use them for.

There are so many ways in which our students can engage with math, and we want our students to feel empowered as decision makers, not daunted by options. It is important to invest time in this stage to familiarize students with the physical space and to clearly introduce each tool and its potential uses. This can look like a ten-minute minilesson or a collective inquiry around how the tool might help accomplish mathematical work and how to handle it safely. Deciding whether to show students directly or allow them to discover depends on whether you want students to do something a particular way that you have predetermined (such as for safety or because of the constraints of your classroom space) or how they do things is open for invention or shared decision-making (for instance, because there are many ways to use pattern blocks or where you keep them is less important than coming to an agreement as a class).

Students need to know what different parts of the classroom can be used for so they can make productive decisions. For instance, you'll want students to be familiar with when and why to use the floor, tables, a quiet corner, or other areas for their work, and discuss how to maintain safe movement throughout the room when people and materials are scattered in many spaces. Similarly, students will need familiarity with where materials are stored and any procedures for accessing them, such as using a caddy or bucket to take some square tiles back to the table.

When a question comes up or a disagreement arises, we want students to be self-directed in choosing a tool or finding a space that will support them in moving forward, something that begins with knowing and understanding their choices. Providing students with choices and then reflecting afterward on the consequences of these choices, however small at first, builds students' capacity to be increasingly independent. Having the familiarity and the vocabulary to name and make these choices for themselves gives students shared ownership of the room for serious mathematical inquiry. By taking the time to introduce all the pieces that comprise the physical environment, we assure our students that this is their space and their tools to use in a way that works best for them.

Provide structured time to explore space and tools.

Children can be so curious, and sometimes the most meaningful learning moments in mathematics stem from an unexpected question or wondering. A student might wonder, "How many cubes can I stick together?" and create their own counting task. Because this curiosity can sometimes feel like getting off track or off task, it is critical that we provide structured time for our students to explore their environment, tools, and all the elements of the physical space, before we tackle more focused mathematical learning. This structured exploration time makes space for their curiosity, while also providing opportunities to collect valuable information that will support their math learning.

The exploration period is important, because even though we may have clear ideas about manipulatives and their specific functions, students need to figure out how they could and want to use manipulatives for themselves by exploring possibilities in both mathematical and nonmathematical ways. For one first grader exploring a rekenrek for the first time, this manifested in four minutes of rubbing the bead frame on their face, and one minute of counting the beads. They needed to see what the tool felt like and what it could do, to understand how they might use it mathematically. Some of the ideas students come up with may not be safe ("How far can I throw this block?"), and the structure and parameters teachers set will support students in taking mathematical risks and indulging wonderings while feeling safe in their environment.

Support students to choose a space to work where they can be productive.

Students need opportunities to try diverse seating options as we guide them in deciding which spot will be the best for working with their partner on particular mathematical tasks. Once students know clearly with whom they are working (something we will discuss a bit later in this chapter), where they sit should be one of the first low-stakes joint decisions they make. During this phase of establishing structure, the novelty of options and decision-making can be both exciting and distracting for many students. There will be some inevitable chaos and conflict and some repeated questioning on our end of whether assigned seats might just be easier for everyone. However, this denies students the opportunity to develop autonomy and decision-making skills and ultimately the opportunity to work in a space and way that works best for them.

Instead of taking back control, teachers can offer specific forms of support for students. Model what it looks like to choose a space, thinking aloud about how you know if the spot you've chosen is or is not going to help you do your best work. You might say, "Maybe the couch in the library is not the best place for me because a lot of children like to work in the library and I know I need a quieter space. Maybe the floor table is the best place for me, because the pillows are comfortable, it's in a quiet corner, and there's room for me and my partner to sit together and work."

These decisions are easier to make when students have a sense for what it feels like to choose the right spot. Teachers might reflect with students, "What does it feel like to be productive?" Students might notice what kinds of spaces allow room for both partners and their materials. What distracts them? What kinds of spaces feel more or less distracting? Teachers and students can then make anchor charts about the different spots, highlighting what's great about each space (see Figure 3.2). Teachers can also confer with student partnerships who are unsure or in conflict about this decision. For instance, if you notice a partnership rise from the rug and then stop, you can ask questions to support their decision-making, such as "What kind of spot do you each need to work? What spots will give you both what you need?"

Interactions with Others

Students need to know what it means to be and have a partner for mathematical work and how to negotiate the initial decisions that go with getting started on tasks that ask them to think together. Students have to make lots of decisions before they even get to mathematical thinking in collaborative classrooms, and we want to support students in learning what those decisions are and how to make them. We will want to keep the following goals in mind:

FIGURE 3.2 Anchor Chart: How to Choose Where to Sit

1. As a class, define what a productive partnership means.
2. Support students in being and choosing a productive partner.
3. Support students with negotiating how to get started with collaboration.

As a class, define what a productive partnership means.

A productive partnership is one in which each partner has a clear role, feels heard, can contribute to and manage the mathematical work, and can resolve disagreements. This is particularly important when we define doing mathematics as having ownership over making sense of mathematical structure and patterns; so what happens when two or more students share that ownership? They must negotiate their choices in productive and inclusive ways, where no student takes over and no one is left out. All ideas are worthy of being taken into consideration. As teachers, we begin this work by defining together what it means to do this work with each other. Just as teachers set norms for other parts of the day, such as read-aloud and sitting at the carpet, we establish clear norms for what being a productive partner looks like, sounds like, and feels like in mathematics. These specific details create an environment where students feel valued and have ownership over their work. Students can return to and reflect on their definition of productive partnerships when things aren't going as planned. Most importantly, students learn how it feels to be in a productive partnership through reflecting on moments when they experienced successful joint work and when they experienced challenges, including moments of distraction, confusion, or domination. In this book, we provide our view of a productive partnership, though your class's homegrown definitions are more valuable because they stem from their lived experiences. Developing a classroom community-driven definition of productive partnership based on those lived experiences takes time.

Research Note **Creating a Culture of Collaboration.** Children can learn to interact with one another in ways that promote robust learning. In one study (Mercer, Wegerif, and Dawes 1999), elementary-aged children were taught to become aware of how they used language to work with one another and to use what the researchers called "ground rules" for collaboration. Ground rules included the following: all relevant information is shared; the group seeks to reach agreement; the group takes responsibility for decisions; reasons are expected; challenges are accepted; alternatives are discussed before a decision is taken; and all in the group are encouraged to speak by group members. When compared with children from a control group, the children who were taught how to interact with others were better able to solve reasoning problems both together and individually.

Support students in being and choosing a productive partner.

Ultimately, across the elementary years, we as teachers want students to figure out how to choose partners for mathematical work. In early grades, students are often not yet ready to make these selections independently but do benefit from conversations about what makes a good partner. For younger students, you could make suggestions about who they might partner with. As students get older, they can take on more responsibility for self-assessing what and who makes a good partner for them, experimenting and learning from the results. To make a decision about who will support learning, we need to help students understand that friends are not always the same people that help them grow as learners. Teachers could support students' decision-making by reflecting with them, asking "What do you want from a partner?," and revisiting your growing definition of a productive partnership. Then invite students to try to find a partner by first thinking about the question, "Who might you be productive with today?" You might let students look around the room to get ideas, keeping in mind what they need from one another. Faith gives students particular prompts to think about, such as "Who might help you? Who could you help?," and then students make lists of potential partners before leaving the carpet to find someone to work with. They will need to approach others and ask if they would like to be partners for the day. Even with proactive work, know that students will struggle to choose a productive partner. They are still likely to choose only their friends. They are also likely to argue with their partner and struggle to make decisions. This is all part of the work. At the end of the work time, invite students to reflect on their partnership and discuss what went well and what they still are working on. Over many days, students will begin to discover qualities they appreciate about their classmates and what they can do to be a productive partner for others.

Support students with negotiating how to get started with collaboration.

It takes a lot of practice to become comfortable with sharing your learning process with another person. If student collaboration is going to be successful, we need to support students by making explicit what such interactions look like in mathematical work. Students need to know how to position their bodies in relation to one another and materials—can both students read the shared poster, take turns, decide on roles (such as who will write or roll the dice), contribute their ideas, and listen to others for understanding? In a class discussion, share that when we collaborate, we need to have eye contact and face our partner. The materials are in between us, accessible to all, and we take turns with materials and jobs. Before stating these behaviors to the class, you might invite students to share what it looks like to work with a partner. Record these behaviors on an anchor chart to revisit when necessary. Then, model for the class with a student partner, and have students practice, too. For instance, Faith might set up a fishbowl with a student partner in the middle, where she turns her back to her partner, freezes the scene, and gets suggestions, from students in the circle observing, on what she could do instead.

We also want to offer opportunities to model what happens when they need to make a decision or they disagree. As Faith described earlier in the chapter, she offers first graders some language for resolving conflict by making suggestions, "Maybe we can . . ." and "What if we . . . ," to support her students in negotiating problem-solving. You might also ask the students how they might approach mathematical or relational conflict, and again ask students to model and rehearse. Support students to use these ideas by writing them on an anchor chart that is visible to the students while they are working. Once they are off working as partners, continue to support this work by noticing and naming their growing skills, such as "I see Jose and Karina facing each other with their notebook in the middle." You might also approach students who need some support and have them rehearse with their partner in the moment. For instance, if you notice one partner shouting "Me first!," you might suggest they try this differently by asking, "What could we ask if you want to go first? Can you try that?" so that students can revise this interaction. Students need a lot of time and support to build these skills, but if we spend time modeling, practicing, and reflecting, students will move more consistently into collaborative behaviors.

In the primary grades, you will find yourself spending a lot of time supporting students with negotiating taking turns and sharing materials. In the intermediate grades, you will find yourself working with students to negotiate who is right and wrong and how to move through disagreements about the mathematics. All of this is to be expected. We want students to productively struggle with these skills.

Interactions with Mathematics

In this stage, as we begin to bring students into mathematical work, the most important thing we can do is establish what doing mathematics means. Your students may have had experiences in previous math classrooms where engaging in mathematics, and being successful, was defined very differently than you hope to in your classroom. This stage includes three goals for developing interactions with mathematics:

1. Begin to define what *doing* mathematics means in your classroom.
2. Send clear messages about what constitutes mathematical success and recognize examples immediately.
3. Establish a clear lesson structure that includes a launch, exploration, and discussion.

Research Note **How Teachers Communicate and Structure Success.** Learning and doing mathematics is a social activity (Lerman 2000). Part of teaching includes defining with and for students what it means to do mathematics in their classroom, especially in classrooms where students play an active role. Yackel and Cobb (1996) have called these ways of doing mathematics a classroom's "sociomathematical norms." They found that classroom teachers can develop powerful sociomathematical norms with students by eliciting student ideas and inviting students to listen to one another, respect one another and themselves, accept different viewpoints, and engage in an exchange of thinking. Similarly, in a review of the research literature, Walshaw and Anthony (2008) found that teachers who (a) listen attentively to students' explanations and questions, (b) ask students to justify their answers (Woodward and Irwin 2005), and (c) ensure that students listen attentively to each other (Nathan and Knuth 2003) developed successful collaborative mathematics classroom cultures.

Begin to define what *doing* **mathematics means in this space.** Students receive many messages during their years of schooling about what doing mathematics means. Perhaps your students learned in the past that doing mathematics means finding answers, completing worksheets, or performing procedures. These definitions of doing math are inadequate and inequitable. Mathematics has *making sense of numbers, data, and space* at the heart. Teachers want to focus on the verbs, the actions that students take individually and collectively, to make sense of mathematics. These actions make up mathematical practices, many of which are reflected in the Common Core State Standards for Mathematical Practice (National Governors Association Center for Best Practices and Council of Chief State School Officers 2010) and in state standards.

Students need to learn to make sense of a mathematics problem, look for patterns and regularity, conjecture and explain their thinking, justify why what they are doing makes mathematical sense, and represent their thinking in ways others can see. They also must learn to revise their thinking, take the ideas of others into consideration, and identify their own confusions, among many other practices. In this stage, you'll need to consider your students' prior experience with these practices and name explicitly what it looks like and sounds like to engage in them. If your students are entirely new to this definition of what it means to do mathematics, then you may want to start with the foundational idea that math is about making sense, and that requires that we struggle, share, and revise our thinking along the way. You can do this by choosing tasks that ask for sensemaking and focusing on student thinking; you'll need to make lots of statements about what you value, such as "Look at all the different ways we found! Do you notice how there is more than just one strategy to solve a problem?" or "Jimena tried one strategy but her answer didn't make sense. She realized she had to revise her work and she went back and tried another strategy and checked her work. Thumbs up if you did the same thing." But if your students have more experience, you can develop more explicit classroom expectations for justification, for example. In this case, you might draw specific attention to a student's explanation during a number talk and point out what made it convincing or ask students to name what about that explanation was most persuasive or clear.

Send clear messages about what constitutes mathematical success and recognize examples immediately.

Hand in hand with what it means to do mathematics is the question of how success is recognized. Many of us can remember math classrooms where success was defined by two behaviors: getting the answer right and doing so quickly (Seeley 2015). Our aim is to disrupt this notion and create a new definition of success, based on engaging in the practices described earlier, such as explaining, justifying, representing, posing questions, making connections, noticing patterns, and persisting through struggle. Students need to see that you value these actions consistently and persistently, particularly in this stage, to redefine their own understanding of success. For instance, we want students to see their struggle as evidence of success, not failure, so they need to hear you explicitly noticing and valuing their struggle before they begin to believe that that struggle is inherently constructive (even when it feels uncomfortable).

When you see students engaged in any act of doing mathematics, even if it is in the earliest stages of development, name what they are doing and why it is important. For instance, students don't learn to explain their thinking all at once. They often start with partial explanations, such as "I put them together." In these moments, before you go on to support the child to add more to their explanation (perhaps by asking, "What did you put together?" or "Why did you put those two groups together?"), you can pause and recognize publicly that this is how explaining begins and this is what mathematicians do.

Changing what it means for students to be successful means that we have to think carefully about what we praise and why, taming the knee-jerk reaction to praise or confirm correct answers or tell students "good job" for doing what we've asked. Instead, we should connect the value in students' efforts and actions not to pleasing us as teachers, but to what it offers learners. Far more useful than "good job" is "The arrows you drew make it really clear how your drawing is connected to the number sentence you wrote. This helps us all understand just what you did." Expect that changing your own habits for recognizing success may be just as hard for you as shifting the definition of doing mathematics is for students.

Establish a clear lesson structure that includes a launch, an exploration, and a discussion.

The routines you use for teaching math need to reflect and support what it means to do math in your classroom. These routines include both the tasks you use and how your structure your time. Decades of mathematics education research have supported a three-part structure for math teaching that sets students up as sense makers and investigators: launch, explore, and discuss. Let's take a look at each part of this structure.

As discussed in Chapter 1, a mathematics lesson needs to include a rich task that your students don't yet know how to solve fluently. This task should require productive struggle of students, because that is where learning happens and your students are capable of making sense. A lesson begins with the teacher presenting this task to students, making sure they understand what the task says and any parameters, and establishing any specific ground rules for the task. This might involve reading the task aloud from a chart or on a projector where everyone can see it and checking to make sure students understand the context or language, if it might be unfamiliar (such as "What is a silo?" or "What does it mean that he *distributed* the cards?"). The teacher then clarifies any expectations that they need to be aware of, such as "Your group needs to make a chart of your process to share with the class at the end" or "I've brought in some metersticks in case anyone would like to use them, and they are on the back table." The launch should take no more than fifteen minutes, but ideally much less, especially with younger students with less stamina for listening to directions.

Then send students off to work collaboratively on the task for the bulk of the class time. Younger students may go off and work for a shorter period, check in as a whole group on how things are going, and then go back to collaborate further. Obviously, this is a complex endeavor that we will devote this book to unpacking, but students at the very beginning of school need to see the need to learn to collaborate in mathematics. If your mathematics structure demonstrates that this is where their time will be spent, it communicates the real need to learn how to make this time productive.

Finally, mathematics should close with a discussion in which the teacher orchestrates learning across the different student experiences that just unfolded side by side during the collaborative work time. There are many ways to use this discussion, and others have written entire books on how to do this well (see Kazemi and Hintz 2014; Smith and Stein 2011). Teachers might ask students to reflect on their partnerships, share their problem-solving strategies or representations, compare and contrast approaches across the classroom, analyze a challenge someone faced, look for patterns, or generalize a mathematical concept or principle. There is much that can be accomplished in a fifteen-minute discussion. In fact, the greatest challenge is often choosing what to focus the conversation on.

Embedded in this structure are messages such as these:

- We all have the power to make sense of mathematics.
- We learn math by talking with each other and exploring ideas.
- We all have ideas that are worthy of consideration.
- We persist in struggle because it leads to learning.
- There are many pathways for solving any problem.
- Math is more about the process than getting the right answer.

You will likely want to say these messages directly to students, over and over, and they will hear you and believe you more readily if your structure for teaching mathematics is sending the same messages every time you do math. If your students have never experienced this structure before—if their prior structure was review homework, watch the teacher model solving two or three problems, independent practice of the same problem type—then you will want to have explicit conversations about what this structure is and its purposes. Expect that students may push back on structures that don't tell them what to do step by step, and they will look to you to explain procedures and confirm right answers. Resist! Remember that you must consistently affirm your belief in the messages above, and if you substitute your own strategies, thinking, and answers for students', you undermine your goal of positioning students as competent and mathematics as something we do together.

Three Tools to Support Your Students in Developing Collaboration

So, how do we help students meet these goals? There are three pedagogical strategies that we use over and over as we support students in moving toward the collaborative goals in this phase and, really, all the phases that follow. We support students in becoming reflective and metacognitive by making this a centerpiece of closing discussions when needed, and we teach students what collaboration looks like and sounds like by acting it out together and recognizing it aloud when we see students moving toward productive work together.

Lead a Reflective Conversation

After students have tried collaborative work, you can focus students' attention on how the collaboration went and whether there were strong bright spots or emergent challenges. Students benefit from learning to reflect on the choices they made and considering what those choices mean for tomorrow. During a closing discussion, you can ask students a general reflection question, or notice something that you saw and invite students to reflect. These questions could sound like:

- "How did your collaboration go today?"
- "What went well in your collaboration today?"
- "Did anyone have any challenges in your collaboration today?"
- "I noticed some challenges with sharing materials today. Did anyone notice the same thing?"

These questions can surface specific challenges or successes and give you opportunities to name specific actions or behaviors that help or hinder collaboration. These might be very specific, such as eye contact or compromising on a place to work, or they could be more challenging such as feeling like a partner was ignoring another's ideas or excluding others from participation. During the conversation you can support students in getting specific about what helps or what they need in collaboration by asking questions like:

- "Did anyone have a partner who helped them ____. What did your partner do?"
- "What made your partnership challenging today? What do you think you needed?"

- "How did you know that your partnership was successful (or working or productive) today? What was going on?"
- "What can we do tomorrow to make our partnerships more successful (or productive)?"

You can name specific actions, language, or behaviors that will help students, drawing on their reflections of what works for them. You might refer to charts you have made as a class (see Figure 3.3), or use this as an opportunity to create one.

> **Research Note The Power of Metacognition.** Metacognition refers to thinking about thinking. When students learn to think about their thinking, they develop more effective work habits and are able to assess their own performance. Reflection helps students develop knowledge about themselves as learners and supports metacognition. Supporting student reflection—including through both written reflections and whole-class conversations—can improve the quality of how students interact with one another (Desautel 2009).

Show Students Ways to Act

Students very likely do not have a vision of how collaboration looks and sounds in action. If there are patterns or common challenges that emerged during work time, you can offer a concrete next step, showing them a way to act on that challenge. Choose a specific aspect of collaboration, like body position or a way to negotiate where to sit, and demonstrate options with and for students. This could look like:

- **Act it out:** As the teacher, say and show exactly what you want students to try.

  - ▶ "One thing we can do when we disagree with our partner is make a suggestion. We can ask, 'Maybe we can . . . ?' Let me show you what I mean."
  - ▶ "When we choose a spot to work we need to . . . Watch me."

- **Fishbowl:** Have two or more students demonstrate a move or behavior so that students can see their peers doing something specific. This can be something you have observed them doing successfully in their collaboration. You can narrate what students are doing that you hope others will try out.
- **Use video:** Record students using a move or action that is useful to their collaboration and share that video with the class, so that you can pause, rewind, and replay it to draw attention to specific aspects.

- **Freeze scenes:** Set up a scenario (perhaps something you observed during work time). Let the scene play out until there's a point in the conflict where a choice can be made (e.g., "I want to hold the pen!" "No, I want to hold the pen!"), then call out "Freeze!" and ask the class to think and talk to a partner, asking "What can they do next?" or "What could they do instead?" Unfreeze the scene, encouraging students to resolve the conflict with one or more of the shared suggestions.
- **Make a chart:** When there are features or options you'd like students to be able to refer to later, making a chart is a useful way of holding onto ideas that come up in discussion. Charts might collect things like ways collaboration looks and sounds, sentence stems for making choices with your partner, or what mathematicians do (see Figure 3.3).

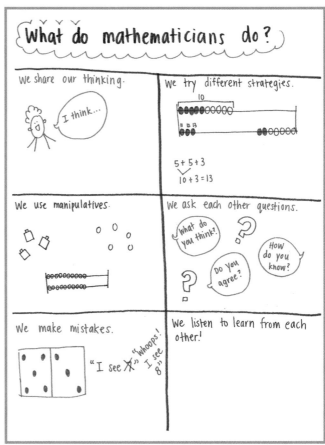

FIGURE 3.3
Anchor Charts Support Students to
Learn How to Act in Collaboration

Say What You See

When a moment comes up that is an example of one of your key messages about interacting with the environment, each other, or mathematics, point it out to students, both to recognize their efforts and also to support others in trying the wonderful things you see. Keep your eye on marginalized students to elevate students who may not have been recognized before.

You might say:

- "I notice Jose and Jordan are facing each other and that helps them to listen."
- "You really struggled with this strategy and you figured it out by . . ."
- "Did you all notice that we found five different ways to solve this problem? There really are so many strategies you can use no matter what the problem is, and your job is to figure out which one makes the most sense to you."

This action can overlap with the other two, leading to a reflective discussion of things you notice or an opportunity for students to fishbowl something you observed that others would benefit from seeing.

Rollout

The nine goals described in this chapter are not a checklist; instead, building students' capacity to navigate interactions with the environment, others, and mathematics requires pushing multiple goals forward simultaneously. In this section, we describe how Faith and Mary roll out the nine goals in their classrooms. We have segmented this phase into three loose stages and labeled them each by weeks for ease, but the amount of time Faith and Mary spend varies depending on their students. Similarly, we have begun with "week 1" to indicate whenever you begin mathematics work, which may not actually be the first week of school.

Because they are different teachers and they teach different grades, their rollout plans have some things in common and some key differences. Each of the stages begins with describing both teachers' shared goals and how they approach making progress toward them. Then, Mary and Faith each describe the work they do with students that is distinct, including the kinds of activities they choose, what they pay attention to and for, and the types of discussions and interactions they foster.

Week 1: Getting Started

In the first week, Faith and Mary both prioritize goals for interacting with the environment and observing students to gather informal assessment data about the ways they interact with one another and mathematics. They provide students opportunities to explore math materials that will be useful in the coming units, such as linking cubes, pattern blocks, base ten blocks, and square tiles. They structure their class time so that there is a launch with the introduction of materials, time for exploration, and then a reflective discussion at the end. Although there is not yet deep mathematical exploration taking place, structuring time in this way establishes the seed of the launch-explore-discuss routine, which they grow over the coming weeks. During this time, they observe their students to learn how they naturally interact with one another, how they engage with the math manipulatives, and what mathematical thinking emerges spontaneously. For instance, some students might make comparisons between different groups of manipulatives, like "My stick is longer than yours," which you could ask questions about (such as "How do you know? How much longer is it? How many more would she need to add to make them equal?"). Similarly, students often use manipulatives to create and extend patterns, which you can ask questions about, such as "I notice there is a pattern to your cubes. What is it?"

During this initial phase, Faith and Mary introduce the ways they expect students to talk about themselves, their thinking, and their choices. In the discussion part of each lesson, Mary and Faith ask students to reflect on their choices, and they position students with the authority to make those choices, by asking questions like "How did things go?" and "How do you know?" Students often struggle to pinpoint how their choices affected them and others, and these conversations help students articulate with increasing precision the consequences of their choices. For instance, students may be able to say that "it was hard" today, and by asking questions, you can support students in figuring out if the challenge had to do with too little space, a noisy environment, or a disagreement with a partner, and in turn, what they (and others) can do about those issues tomorrow. Together through discussion in mathematics and throughout the school day, the class develops shared vocabulary for what it means to be safe and productive.

By focusing on how to make choices in the environment, such as where to sit and how to use tools safely, Mary and Faith establish norms that support them in moving into more mathematical work, while surfacing issues that can be addressed early, such as competing for coveted spots in the room. Mary and

Faith don't linger in this initial stage. Allowing students to explore and play with manipulatives for too long can create new management issues down the road. Instead, ensure some norms about safety and gather the data you need to continue to tackle issues as you move forward.

First Grade: FAITH

Beginnings are exciting, especially in first grade. I start our work by naming our excitement and engaging in conversations about how we can be excited, and be curious, but most importantly be safe. We spend time co-constructing norms around safety, first thinking about what makes us feel unsafe: others grabbing things out of our hands, yelling, throwing, hitting, fighting. We talk about why we wouldn't want to do those things, how it makes us feel if others were to do those things, and how when we don't feel safe, we can't be curious and we can't be excited about the work we're doing. We co-create agreements and continue to reflect on them after every work period. Embedded in these conversations around safety, where we talk, act out, and think aloud through different scenarios, is implicit trust building. I know this time invested in ensuring everyone is being safe is laying the foundation for collaboration and mutual trust.

As we continue to engage in reflective conversations about safety, I deliberately introduce a new manipulative each day (being mindful of what might be helpful in the first unit and what won't), building stamina for being on the carpet (both during the launch portion of the math block when I introduce a new manipulative and during the reflective discussion at the end of our work time), and co-creating norms for sharing space and materials. As students explore, I walk around and loudly notice when partnerships are taking turns with materials, putting things in the middle, asking each other questions, and practicing our co-constructed agreements. This phase can be brief, but it is critical in setting the tone for productive collaboration. I do not linger in this phase because the work time of exploring a new manipulative each day without a mathematical task can move quickly from curious exploration to play in a way that's hard to wrangle once it's time to really engage with math and sensemaking.

Fourth Grade: MARY

I start our work by introducing the word *productive*. I intentionally set the foundation that students are responsible for their productivity and should be consistently reflecting on how they are engaging with the work of the day. This happens outside of my math time during my morning meeting. I end my morning message with "Let's have a productive day." During the meeting, we talk through what it means to be productive and why it is important. I want to make sure students can define the word and know what it looks like in a classroom. At this stage, it is a general conversation about productivity. It isn't until week 2 or 3 that I align this definition to our math work.

Our first math routine is a dot talk. This strategy is often seen in the primary grades, but I've found that it is a great way both to establish my math talk norms and to emphasize the importance of explaining your strategy over getting the answer. We do a dot talk every day, progressing to more challenging images. The goal is for students to see the value in listening to other people's strategies, seeing mistakes as a learning opportunity, and sharing multiple strategies. My students love dot talks, and as the year goes on and we transition to number talks, they always ask to do more dot talks.

Weeks 2–3: Number Talks and Building Partnership Skills

In the next two weeks, Faith and Mary begin to tackle goals for interacting with mathematics through number talks and lay a foundation for interacting with others, drawing on their observations from the first week. A central focus at this time is pressing students to explain their mathematical thinking and learning to attend to one another's ideas. Number talks are the vehicle for these goals at this time, because they can be relatively brief and can precede launching a full math unit. Each number talk is a rehearsal for how students explain thinking, how we each listen to and question one another's ideas, and what constitutes convincing evidence. At the same time, Mary and Faith can use the number talks to gather informal assessment data on their students' understanding of number concepts. In conjunction with number talks, both teachers continue to support students in learning about mathematical materials and ways they can use the classroom environment to work in math.

In the final few days before launching the first math unit, the teachers begin to discuss what it means to be a productive partner or in a productive partnership. Together the class builds anchor charts describing what it means to be productive and what students need from each other to make a partnership work. For instance, partners may need eye contact to know they are being listened to, materials positioned between one another for access, or their partner making suggestions rather than decisions. This focus represents a shift from how partners share space or materials to how partners share thinking and work together toward solving problems. How Mary and Faith do this varies, in large part because their students are at very different developmental stages. You'll notice that Faith supports her first-grade students with language for sharing ideas, and Mary's fourth graders can articulate directly who they are and what they need as mathematicians. This work sets the stage for launching the first math unit.

First Grade: FAITH

Now that we've grown familiar with the structure of our math block and our rug time stamina has increased, I introduce a dot talk routine as the first part of our launch. My goals for dot talks in these first few weeks is to demonstrate the value of multiple strategies, support students in the practice of listening to and orienting to one another's thinking, and both model and offer structured opportunities to practice explaining their mathematical thinking to others. I introduce the concept of think time, and we engage in discussions about why it's important to give ourselves and others think time. I start to introduce words like *agree*, *disagree*, and *revise*, as I revoice their thinking.

In week 3, we build on the norms we've created around sharing space and materials, and I introduce the question, "How do we collaborate in math?" These norms of collaboration continue to iterate as a living chart, as we generate ideas about what it means to work together, building on things we notice make our partnerships successful and what we could do differently when they aren't. Some of these norms continue to be about sharing materials ("We put our materials in the middle") or physical orientation ("We sit side by side"). But the real work of thinking about how we collaborate in math begins when we butt up against a problem, "What if we don't agree on what to do?" or "What if we both want to go first?" In this phase, we really engage with ideas about how we can negotiate productively toward the work of collaboration. We practice saying things like "Maybe we can . . . ?" when we disagree, and "Do you agree?" to ensure we're on the same page (see "Notes from the Classroom" on pages 35–36 for an example).

Fourth Grade: MARY

In week 2, I focus on redefining success in math and what it means to be good at math. First, I do this through helping students to understand growth mindset. We do a series of lessons where we explore the science of learning—how our brain changes when we make mistakes. My students come to me with mathematical identities that have developed over the course of their first four years of learning at school. Part of this can include a rigid belief about what success in math looks like, with one way to get to a correct answer. In this series of lessons, I really push the students to begin to see mistakes as part of the learning process and something that we hope for every day. We read *Your Fantastic, Elastic Brain* by JoAnn Deak to learn about how our brains grow and change. We watch videos of mathematicians talking about their work and a clip from *Sesame Street* called "The Power of Yet" by Janelle Monae (see https://www.youtube.com/watch?y=XleUyZyuvAs). During these lessons, I open with either reading a book or watching a video to start a conversation. Then, I have the students engage with either a partner conversation or a task where they apply the learning from that day. For example, on the day we watch a video that shows what happens when synapses fire, students go off and color an image of a brain with synapses firing and they label the synapse with a mistake they made recently. I want to make sure we spend time discussing the science of learning and engage in a task that supports students to apply their learning.

The lessons that follow explore what math is and what mathematicians do. We start by cocreating an anchor chart titled "What Is Math?" My goal here is to orient students to being reflective about what they know to be true about math. Then, we read picture books about mathematicians that will help us understand what skills and habits mathematicians hold. We do this for several days until I feel like students are starting to shift their definition of success in math. I intentionally choose books that show mathematicians that are women and people of color to also support students to see that everyone can be a mathematician. During these lessons, we also watch videos of mathematicians talking about math, and then we discuss how passionate and excited they are about their field. All along the way, we are adding to and revising our "What Is Math?" anchor chart.

In these weeks I transition from doing dot talks to number talks to deepen student comfort with mistakes, develop their capacity for explaining their thinking, and begin the work of students engaging with each other's ideas. Once numbers are involved, there is more resistance, because number talks favor those students with greater facility with numbers, and those that have less facility often fall silent. As the facilitator, I have to be very patient and wait as students productively struggle with explaining their thinking. I am also intentional with whom I call on because I want to make sure that I am not continuing previous hierarchies of who has the right answer. Some students are eager to share their thinking, and this eagerness can oftentimes shut down the students who process information at a slower rate. I want to make sure my students know that speed is not the defining characteristic of success in math. I pick numbers that students might have an easier time engaging with so that there is time for the students to transition from explaining how they saw the dots in the dot talks we did previously to composing and decomposing numbers in number talks.

In week 3, I introduce the mathematical concept of decomposing numbers. We do an activity where I introduce friendly number pairs for students to begin to see that they have different preferences and relationships to numbers. I ask the students to think of ten and then to think of how they would break the ten into two numbers. They do this with linking cubes to slow what their preference is, and then we make an anchor chart of all the options for friendly number pairs for ten. This work supports students to begin to identify what they need as mathematicians and to support that there are many ways to solve problems.

Weeks 3–4: Introducing the First Math Unit

By introducing the first math unit, we begin to stretch students' thinking and focus more heavily on goals for interacting with mathematics and with others during problem-solving. When launching this first unit, Mary and Faith both deepen the launch-explore-discuss routine through problem-solving, with a particular focus on the explore stage of each lesson. Until now, students have used the explore time to investigate materials without specific mathematical concept goals. With tasks that have clear outcomes and require mathematical struggle, students will need to learn how to use the exploration part of each lesson differently, working toward making sense of tasks and persevering through struggle. To do so, students need to understand what the task is and the expectations for what they might produce during the work time. Students need clarity about what this work time should look and sound like, including how and when they should seek the support of the teacher. In launching the unit that you selected in phase 1 (see Chapter 2), invest time in developing students' understanding of the context of the unit so they can use it to reason more independently about the concepts involved. For instance, Faith often begins the year with a unit that centers on a sleepover where children are moving between the top and bottom bunks on a bunk bed (Fosnot 2007). Faith spends time with the read-aloud story that accompanies the unit, ensures that students all know what a *bunk bed* and *sleepover* are, and can imagine how a two-row rekenrek could model the situation, so that they can work on the tasks with meaning and increasing independence.

Mary and Faith both use this time to support students to transfer some of the skills they have been developing in dot or number talks into partner work, such as listening to one another's ideas. During the work time, both teachers confer with students, coaching them to explain their own and attend to one another's thinking, along with jointly making sense of the task. While conferring, Mary and Faith both ask questions to scaffold these explanations (such as "What did you do first?") and ask reflective questions to support students in attending to one another's thinking (such as "What did you hear your partner say?"), much as they might in a number talk.

For both Faith and Mary, the discussion portion of each lesson begins with reflecting on interactions with each other. By starting the year with a unit that revisits and extends key concepts from the previous grade, students can devote more energy to developing routines and strategies for collaboration. During closing discussions, both teachers pose questions like "How did it go today? How do you know? How productive was your partnership? What does this tell us about what we need from each other or what we can do to make our partnerships productive?" These discussions typically raise issues about collaboration that the class can name and propose potential solutions for the next day, such as how to negotiate turn taking or what strategy to use for problem-solving. Discussions still include, as a second priority, discourse about the mathematical task of the day. Some of students' collaborative challenges stem from challenges with mathematics, as when two partners understand the task differently and splinter into parallel work when they do not yet have the skill to compare and evaluate multiple methods. Addressing conceptual and strategic understandings will, then, also support partner work.

First Grade: FAITH

Ultimately, weeks 3 and 4 are about planting seeds of strategies and behaviors that students can internalize that will serve them in subsequent units. When I launch this first unit, my goal is to situate the heart of the struggle and work in orienting to each other's thinking and ideas. I intentionally begin with a unit where the mathematical concepts are familiar, like combinations of numbers less than ten, which is a kindergarten standard (see Chapter 2 for more on choosing the first unit). In these weeks of the first unit, we gradually spend longer chunks of time on the rug both during the launch and the discussion. We start to shift from merely exposing them to the kind of interactional mathematical language that I hope to be hearing, to providing opportunities to practice that language and set norms around how we talk about the math, our thinking, and each other's thinking. For instance, we do a fishbowl as part of our launch, where a partnership, Jimena and Eva, engage in the work of the day, making different combinations of 8 on the rekenrek. After Jimena shares their thinking ("If you put 5 on the top and 3 on the bottom that makes 8"), then I freeze the partnership and ask the group how Eva could ask a question to learn more about her thinking. They offer questions like "How do you know?" or "How did you get 8?" Chorally we practice "How do you know?" then I unfreeze the partnership and Eva asks that same question to listen and learn from Jimena's thinking.

The launch and the discussion provide opportunities to experience and engage with the language and the math in ways that are efficient, effective, and mutually comprehensible. We define mathematical success as listening to understand, checking our own understanding, sharing our mathematical ideas, and making sure others understand and are learning from us too. Undergirding my focus in this unit is a hope that my students grow interested in sharing ideas in a way that people understand and can learn from, not just sharing for talking's sake. Through the launch, partner work, and discussion, students become familiar with each other's strategies and I intentionally name those strategies, being thoughtful about what strategies are highlighted and facilitating conversations about what makes a strategy effective and efficient. For instance, I will name when I notice students are counting on, and during discussion, I ask students to think, turn, and talk about whether it is quicker to start with 5 and count on 6, 7, 8, or start with 3 and count on 4, 5, 6, 7, 8. After we name, think through, and practice the strategy collectively, I give the students an opportunity to reflect on the strategy, asking for a thumbs up if they think they will try the counting on strategy themselves. This is the beginnings of students planning what strategy they will try that day and thinking about the effectiveness and efficiency of that strategy.

During the exploration, I walk around and check in with partnerships. I confer to support productive partnerships, but also to model and practice talk moves to orient toward each other's thinking while jointly engaging in sensemaking. In addition to partnership conferences, I also use the exploration time to get a sense of the larger needs of the group. What are many partnerships doing well? What do many partnerships struggle with or need more support with? What would be a high-leverage strategy or topic of conversation to bring to the whole-group discussion? If many students are checking their work by recounting the beads one by one, but some are noticing the friendly chunk of five, then counting on from there, I would spend conferring time naming that strategy, asking if they could share what they did, and jointly rehearsing a share of their strategy to bring to the whole group. This doesn't mean that I expect all students to start finding their friend five and counting on, but having students share the strategy reinforces the work of orienting to each other's thinking, and developing routines and strategies for sensemaking and collaboration.

Fourth Grade: MARY

During this first unit, it is important to begin dismantling hierarchies that are built into student mathematical identities from previous years. I use two central strategies to disrupt existing patterns of engaging in math. First, I shift the mathematical work into a context, which supports students to be more interested in their problem-solving and helps to dismantle the idea that there are the students who are "good at math." Second, I promote students' mathematical authority by resisting telling them what to do and whether they are right. Students need to determine what makes sense. For instance, students will come up to me and say, "I don't get this" before attempting a strategy like rereading the problem, talking about the problem with a partner, or picking a strategy. The goal of these weeks is for students to start building skills of wanting to navigate problem-solving on their own, rather than waiting or asking the teacher for help.

My first math unit is a context-based problem where a child starts a T-shirt business and he uses addition and subtraction to manage his business (Fosnot 2007) (see Chapter 2 for more on choosing a first unit). You might remember this context from my "Note from the Classroom" at the beginning of the chapter. Understanding the context of this unit is essential for the students to be able to use the story as a tool for problem-solving. Because of this, we spend a significant amount of time reading the story, comprehending the arc of the story, the story problems that arise, and potential math inquiries that could come from the story. One major goal is for students to be able to retell the story independently because relating back to the story will support them if they get confused or stuck. I have students retell in turn-and-talks and then a few students have the opportunity to retell to the whole group while I act it out. Retelling the story is essential to ensuring students have the tools they need to push through the mathematical struggles they will likely have, because the mathematics is often in the action of the story, like when T-shirts are sold, counted, or added to the inventory.

My main goal of this unit is to support students to build an understanding for what constitutes success in math. In our community of learners, math success looks like grappling with the math and making mistakes. When I see students doing this I name it, "Wow, ____ is really trying to figure this problem out" or "Show me a thumbs up if you made a mistake today. Congratulations, your brain grew today!" I want my students to begin to get comfortable with three things: shifting the focus from the answer to the process of problem-solving, gaining comfort with multiple strategies being valued, and taking the time they need to solve the problem. We talk a lot about how it takes a different amount of time for people to solve the problem because we all process information at different rates and some strategies take longer than others. The discussion often focuses on what mistakes students made and what they learned from their mistakes. By having this conversation, students are also given the opportunity to see other strategies that they might want to try. This work leads to students being self-directed and not depending on teacher support when they are grappling with both the collaboration and mathematics. Students really struggle with not being validated for having the right answer because they are so used to being in an answer-driven math community. During the discussion when students ask if they got it right, I always redirect the question to the community by saying, "What do you all think? Is ___ the answer?" I do this to support students to build confidence in their problem-solving abilities. Or when a student has an answer, I will say, "Hmm, interesting. How do you know that is right?" instead of telling them they have the right or wrong answer. This is ongoing work that continues throughout the year—some students will lean into this work and some will grapple all year with becoming their authority with the mathematics.

As we get further into the unit, I want students to begin to make connections between strategies. This is something that students will work on all year, but it is important that from the beginning students see that the work they are doing is connected. During the exploration, I circulate. I sit down next to a partnership, listen in to their conversation, and then I say something like "What are you working on?" My goal in these conferences is to clearly understand where each students' understanding is with the math concept and the effectiveness of their collaboration and strategy. To support students to see how different strategies are related, I ask questions like "How are your strategies related? How do your strategies both connect to the story? How do your tallies relate to the T-shirts Sami drew?" After I have supported students to connect two strategies, I will often ask those students to share during our discussion. During this phase, I usually ask students to share ahead of time because I want to make sure students have the skills to make connections between strategies before they speak in front of their peers. We are working toward students sharing their strategies and making connections in the discussion without the need for me to facilitate a conference, but they are not yet ready to do this work.

Questions to Consider as You Plan Your Rollout

Here are a few questions you might think through as you map your own way to roll out the goals in this phase with your specific students in your context.

- Who are my students and what do I know about their behaviors and personalities?

  ▶ Are there challenges I can anticipate? How comfortable are they with struggle? What level of messiness/chaos can the class handle?

  ▶ What collaboration have my students experienced in the past? What has math looked like for my students in the past?

  ▶ How do my students think about themselves as mathematicians?

- What other kinds of interactions happen across the day that I can draw on in math?

  ▶ What norms do we have that can carry into math?

  ▶ What language do we have that can support our math work together?

- What forms of independence do I need students to have immediately so we can do other kinds of work together?

- What do I want to learn about my students as mathematicians immediately?

Reflecting Along the Way

As you roll out these goals with your students, pay close attention to how things are going, your growing trust for students, and what they may be struggling with. We've found these reflection questions to be useful tools, and they can also support reflective conversations with your colleagues as you co-plan or learn together.

Reflecting on Interactions with the Environment

- How are students moving around the classroom and accessing materials?

  - What seems to be working smoothly?
  - Are there any traffic jams or places of tension that might require reorganization?
  - Have any safety issues come up that might necessitate more explicit teaching about materials or expectations?

- Are students making productive choices about where to work?

  - Do they seem aware of what works for them?
  - How can you help students be reflective about what works for them and what does not?
  - Have students found new uses for spaces that you'd like to highlight for others?

- Do students seem to know how to use the materials you have made available?

  - What other experiences with materials might they need to make use of them as math tools?
  - Do you students need more time to explore math tools? When might you be able to provide time for unstructured exploration?
  - Have students discovered innovative ways to use tools that you'd like to highlight for others?

Reflecting on Interactions with Others

- Are students orienting to one another in their partnerships?

  - Are they asking one another questions?

- Are they sharing space and materials?
- Are they working in parallel?
- How are they negotiating sharing or turn taking?
- How long is it taking for partners to settle into mathematical work together?
- What challenges are students grappling with in getting into mathematical work together that you might want to reflect on as a class?

- How are students choosing their partners, if you've invited them to do so?

  - Are students only choosing their friends?
  - Are students beginning to choose partners based on who they work well with?
  - How might you highlight the distinction between choosing a math partner and choosing a friend?

- How are students reflecting on their partnerships?

  - Are they able to name what a productive partnership looks, sounds, and feels like?
  - Are they able to name what is working or not working for them as learners?
  - What examples of productivity in partner work do you see that you might highlight for the class?

Reflecting on Interactions with Mathematics

- What messages have you been sending about what math is or what doing math means? Do your messages match your intent?
- How are students doing math?

  - Are they focused on the process or the answers?
  - Are you noticing any anxiety about correctness or risk-taking?
  - How does their engagement with math align with your goals?
  - Where might they need some explicit conversations about doing math or what success looks like?

- How is your math routine going?

  - How different is this routine from your students' prior experiences in mathematics? What might support them in shifting into a new routine?

- Does the routine feel established, or are there parts where you think everyone needs more practice? What kind of practice might they benefit from?
- Are the tasks you are choosing rich enough? Are students struggling productively, stuck, or finishing fast?

If . . . Then . . .

In this section we offer some thoughts on common situations that arise during this phase of establishing your mathematics structure.

If students are struggling to get started on the mathematical work, then . . .

Ask students, "How are you doing?" Notice aloud for students the struggles voiced in their responses. Is the struggle in the task—too difficult or too easy? The math? The partnership? At times, you may realize that the task was not well suited to students' needs, particularly if you notice challenges getting started or engaged across a wide swath of students. If the task is the barrier, try a modified task the next day. At other times the struggle is relational. Engage students in reflective conversation focused on students' naming the tensions or conflict and brainstorming ways to resolve them. Ask them, "What's one thing you could try?"

If you send students off to work and they simply wait for you, then . . .

First, gauge how many of your students are waiting for you, not engaged in meaningful work. If it's a critical mass, consider bringing students back to the rug and clarify the task. You can have a partnership model how to get started, while you voice over what you see the students do, such as "Notice how Riham and Jimena are quickly choosing their best working spot. They're getting the materials they need, deciding how they want to work together, and getting right to work. Thumbs up if you and your partner can do the same thing." Alternatively, you could seize the opportunity to launch a conversation about what we can do as mathematicians when we don't know what to do.

If, on the other hand, there are just a few students waiting, approach them and point out what you notice and what you expect, such as "I see that you're both sitting here and you haven't gotten started. I expect that you will. I'll come back to check on you once I see that you are doing that." Be clear about what you reasonably expect students to be able to do independently at this point and don't step in to do for or with them what you believe they are ready to do on their own. At the beginning of the year, it is critical that students don't become dependent on you to guide them through and validate every decision.

If students race to finish quickly, turn the mathematical work into a competition, or focus only on the answer, then . . .

Ignore the answer and press on with questions about their process and reasoning. Do not validate any correct answers that students have produced. You might say explicitly, "I'm not concerned about the answer. It's your thinking that matters. Tell me what you did and why it makes sense" or "I notice that you have turned this into a race. When you speed through the work, you can't do deep thinking. Mathematicians think slowly and carefully." Ask questions about their reasoning, and if they struggle to provide it, make developing reasoning their task. If students have only answers on their papers and no evidence of their process, press them to develop a way to show what they did that they can explain to you or others. In the whole-group discussion, be sure to highlight examples of partners who did focus on their process and what everyone can learn from their work. You may want to avoid discussing the answers at all at this stage, to continue to reduce the focus on answers, speed, and correctness.

If students only use a previously learned algorithm or are not willing to generate new or multiple strategies, then . . .

Create a need to develop new strategies. There are a few factors to consider when deciding how to do this. First, are students using their chosen algorithm accurately? If not, then this lack of accuracy is motivation for something new. You might say, "I notice that this algorithm is not working for you. It's time to try something new. Let's go back to the problem and think together about what is happening." Second, is the issue pervasive in your class? If you notice most students reverting to the algorithm, you might design a task that asks students to make sense of an example of an error with the algorithm and develop proof with manipulatives.

Alternatively, if it is only a small number of students and they are using the algorithm accurately, two avenues are open. Ask students to explain how the algorithm works and why it makes sense. Invite them to use pictures and manipulatives to do this. If they cannot (or will not), you can choose to say that students can only use methods in math that they can explain, and until they can explain the algorithm, they will need to try something else. Another option is to change the numbers involved in the task, for these students only, such that the algorithm is cumbersome. This might involve choosing numbers with lots of regrouping, those where another method would be much more efficient, or numbers large enough that students do not yet know how to use the algorithm. One final approach is to ask students to do the task in their heads, like a number talk. This might mean making the numbers involved smaller. When students do the work mentally, they are far less likely to set up an algorithm and more likely to think it through by decomposing or visualizing the numbers. If you can get students talking about what they did in their heads, then you can point out that these strategies work on paper, too, and are just the kind of thing you value because they make sense. In the whole-group discussion, be sure to explicitly highlight the strategies that students invent and refine that are grounded in sensemaking.

If students are struggling to explain their thinking, becoming frustrated, or giving up, then . . .

Validate their frustration and support them in breaking their thinking into parts they can explain. Some students will benefit from scaffolding the process by focusing on the steps they used, one by one, while others will find it easier to explain using pictures, diagrams, or manipulatives. You might say, "This struggle that you're in right now is what learning feels like. Figuring out how to explain our thinking is exactly the hard work that we all want to be doing now. So let's take it one bit at a time. What did you think first when you read this task?" or you might ask, "Can you show me what you did? What came first?" As students begin to show you what they have done, you can pause to ask questions about why they made those choices. You can revoice what they have said to you, so that they can hear what putting these ideas together sounds like in an explanation. Keep in mind that every step forward from frustration and giving up matters. Even if students do not develop full explanations at the beginning, any explanation is growth and should be celebrated. If you are using number talks, invite students to revoice one another's explanations to get practice with explaining, tracking the process of problem-solving, and coupling steps with reasoning.

If the classroom feels too chaotic to think, then . . .

Call the class to attention and return everyone to the carpet to reflect on what was happening. Ask questions to help students name what was going on and how it affected their thinking, partnership, or work. You might ask, "I noticed that a few minutes ago it was very noisy, and I couldn't hear Marcus explain his thinking. What was our classroom like for you? How did it affect your work?" Be clear that this is not a moment for accusations, but a time to reflect on the environment that the class was creating together. Ask, "What do we need the classroom to be like so that we can think and work with our partners?" Encourage students to revisit what they need from the environment and each other. If you have made a chart of these features, refer to it. You might invite partners to turn and talk about what they are going to do when they return to work to make sure that we all have a productive environment. Send students back to work a few partnerships at a time. Notice aloud those behaviors that are supportive, such as moving safely, quiet conversation, and getting started on mathematical work. Be sure to return to this moment in the closing discussion to reflect on how things went for everyone after this reset, and the next day remind students in the launch of all the things they did that contributed to a productive learning environment.

If students are choosing places to work, materials, or partners that don't help them get going with math work, then . . .

Notice aloud for students the choices they have made and the effect of those choices. This might sound like "I notice that you've chosen to work together today. Yesterday your partnership was not productive, and I see that you haven't started with the task." Ask students if these choices are working. This could sound like "Is this partnership working for you?" Support students in either making different choices or making a plan for how to make these choices work. If the issue is safety, then you may need to step in and insist they make different choices.

If students are constantly seeking your intervention, then . . .

At the launch of activity, review with students how to seek your intervention and how often they can seek you for a given task. For instance, you might develop a norm that students should not interrupt you when you are conferring with other students or you may develop a signal, like a red plastic cup on the tabletop, that students can use to signal they would like your support when you are available. You may also want to encourage students to ask for support from those outside their partnership if you are not available. Help students make plans for seeking help and resources from peers and independently. During work time, if students continue to come up to you in ways that disrupt your ability to work with other partnerships, state to the class that you are noticing this pattern, and ask students how they might solve their problems.

If students argue with each other, then . . .

Students argue. Arguments are developmentally appropriate and will happen in every classroom every day. Creating an argument-free classroom is not the goal. However, our goal is to teach students skills for navigating arguments in a community of learners and moving past an argument into productive work together. When students are partnered to make joint decisions, they will necessarily disagree some of the time. In these moments, resist the urge to tell students what to do and resolve the dispute by fiat. Instead, allow students the time to sort out the root cause of the dispute to learn how to do so. You may need to describe aloud the conflict you see to help students orient to this root cause and come up with ways to solve it. This experience can serve as a reference in the future for ways to solve disputes.

If students are in a difficult partnership, then . . .

Some students simply do not work well together, whether they quickly turn to play or conflict. Sometimes arguments become such a consistent pattern that a particular partnership is never able to move toward productivity. We want to acknowledge that not all students can work with everyone equally well and partnerships often need to be strategic around social issues. That said, one unproductive and inequitable pattern we have seen in classrooms is to partner a boy with challenging behavior with an organized, quiet girl, who we expect will manage the partnership. Although this may appear to work, it perpetuates problematic gender roles and an inequitable distribution of work. So, what to do? Ask yourself questions: "What is the purpose of the partnership today? What partnership goals do I have for these students in the long run? When might I have seen these students working with others in productive ways? With whom? This might have been on the playground, during literacy work, or after school. Who else struggles with similar partnership skills? What could they learn by grappling with their struggles together, rather than being partnered with someone who will simply take care of these issues for them?" If you have given students the autonomy to select their own partners, then you may want to use some of these questions individually with the students in the difficult partnership to reflect on working with others and generate new potential partnership ideas. If not, you can use these reflective questions yourself to try to assign a new partner with a better likelihood of working productively.

Signs to Celebrate

Celebrating progress toward your goals is critical for your community to grow. Recognize small steps that accumulate into the community you and students are striving for together, just as Faith recognized an early use of suggestion language as progress in the story at the opening of this chapter. The list of signs to celebrate at this, or any, stage is endless, but we'd like to draw your attention to a few signals that you might see that indicate your collaborative classroom is under construction:

1. Students are using and exploring tools safely.
2. Students can describe what's not working in the classroom or in their partnerships, even if they don't yet know how to get things back on track.
3. Students can engage in reflection about their collaborations and work.
4. Students are excited about using mathematical strategies of their own choosing, even if they are still driven to find the "right" answer.
5. Students are becoming aware of their mathematical thinking, noticing the choices they made and the processes they used.
6. Students are beginning to explain their mathematical thinking with teacher questions as a scaffold.
7. Students are taking turns and solving some of the challenges for getting started in joint work.
8. Students position their bodies and work so that shared work is possible.
9. Your math class regularly includes a launch, explore, and discussion.

10. You are beginning to trust students' choices and follow their thinking.
11. Your classroom feels a bit messy, a little noisy, with lots of different things happening simultaneously, and you don't need to control it all.
12. You are trying new things and sometimes they feel comfortable.

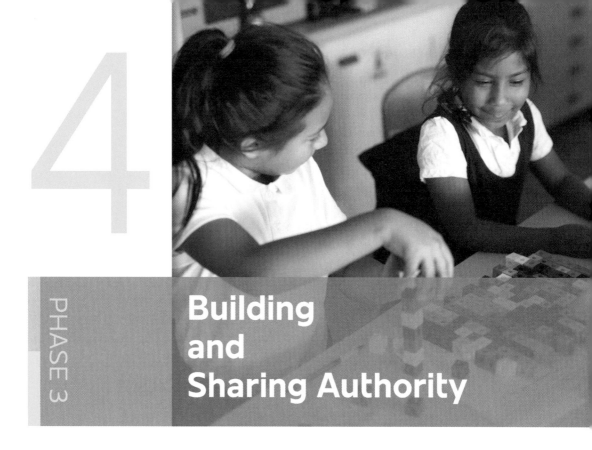

Building and Sharing Authority

Notes from the Classroom

FAITH: "So, I Heard You Say . . ."

I watched Jose and Joanna working on the rug. They were sitting side by side, as they'd been reminded by their peers during the launch. But instead of huddled together using red and green cubes to figure out how many different combinations of 10 red and green apples they could make, they had divided up the cubes and were silently linking different combinations on their own. When I approached them, they were both excited to share what they'd been working on, quickly talking over each other before I gently asked them to pause. I looked at their connected cubes and noticed that they'd made several identical combinations, but that each had also made some combinations that the other had not.

I realized, even after multiple conversations on the rug about what collaboration looks like ("We put our materials in the middle!" "We sit side by side!") and what collaboration sounds like ("We ask each other questions." "We share our ideas."), the students needed something more concrete. We agreed as a class that we would ask each other questions and share ideas, but why? And how?

I drew Jose and Joanna's attention to their partner's combinations, moving their piles closer together, excitedly asking if they noticed how many more they made putting their work together, than if they'd been working alone. With our few remaining minutes, I coached them through sharing their combinations with each other, and practiced with them probing and revoicing after their partner had shared, to make sure they had heard and *understood* what their partner had said ("How do you know?" "So I heard you say . . . Is that right?"). There was a "yes" and a smile, and I prompted the sharing partner to ask if their partner agreed that they had made a unique combination of 10 red and green apples ("Do you agree?"), and we celebrated the "Jose and Joanna red and green apple combination," placing it in the center. I knew this routine needed to be shared, and practiced, and modeled, and practiced some more.

MARY: Reflecting on Unproductive Moments

Between conferring with partners, I stood at the back of my classroom observing the work time. There was a lot going on: it was quite loud and I could see linking cubes in the air and being rolled on the floor. There was some work happening, but there were also a lot of other things happening. I knew that the class was grappling with being productive in their partnerships. I could redirect them, I could end the work time, or I could wait to discuss what was happening during our discussion that day. I knew that redirecting them was very unlikely to be successful. I knew that ending the work time would stop the current challenge, but it wouldn't lead to this happening less often. I decided to let the class continue to be somewhat productive in hopes that we could have an authentic conversation about their unproductiveness and support them with how to be more productive tomorrow. When we sat down at the carpet, I asked the class, "How'd it go today?"

It was silent for an uncomfortable amount of time. Finally, a student said, "Bad. It went bad."

I said, "Can you be more specific? What felt bad today?"

"My partner wasn't working and he was distracting me."

"Who else feels like today was unproductive?" Most of the students nodded. I knew talking about how bad it felt wasn't going to lead to students being more successful, so I decided to ask what did work. "What did go well today?" Again silence, but I waited.

Eventually, a student said, "Me and my partner worked side by side and didn't get distracted by what other kids were doing."

"Yeah, me too. We solved the problem."

So we dug into what these partnerships did. "Melvin, what helped you and your partner to not be distracted? What did you do?" The rest of the discussion was about decisions the partnerships made to help them deal with distractions. Not only did we now have a frame of reference for how to be successful with distractions, our conversation also positioned students, not me, as the ones to solve problems that arose. The next day in the launch, I reminded students of the conversation we had and presented a chart, titled "How to Be Productive with Distractions," that listed the ways they were successful the day before. We now had the memory of the conversation and the chart to support us when another day filled with distractions arose.

n the previous chapter, you learned about nine goals that help foster a collaborative structure and saw some ways to begin establishing that structure. Now that a structure is in place to enable students to do mathematics together, we must ensure that we provide carefully designed opportunities for students to build authority as they navigate interactions with their environment, with others, and with mathematics with less teacher support. Students should feel emboldened to choose tools, materials, and mathematics strategies that will or could work for them in the moment. Students need norms and routines that will support them in communicating their thinking, listening to each other, making sense of one another's thinking, resolving conflict, and making decisions.

Building student authority not only enables students to engage in important learning processes such as reasoning and sensemaking, it also positions students as powerful learners and doers of mathematics and members of a mathematical community. When we work to build student authority, we foster both robust learning and identity development in the classroom.

In this chapter, we'll look at eight new goals that will help you to support students' collaborative efforts by eliciting, listening to, naming, and legitimizing the ideas and choices they're making and providing norms and routines to support mathematics sensemaking among peers. In "Research Notes," we unpack the connections between authority, mathematics learning, and students' identities; the value of eliciting student thinking; and the impacts of centering students' intent in linguistically diverse classrooms.

Goals for Building Authority

In this phase, goals around interactions with the environment begin to recede as students become more skilled in making their own use of the space and materials, while interactions with mathematics and with others come to the fore (see Figure 4.1). As students dig into juicy mathematical ideas and work, the mathematics itself begins to drive the goals we have for collaboration.

	Goals for Interactions With . . .		
	Environment	**Others**	**Mathematics**
PHASE 3 Building and Sharing Authority	• Support students to choose tools, materials, and strategies that could work for them in the moment.	• Establish routines that support students in listening to and making sense of each other's thinking. • Redirect decision-making to partners or peers. • Build tools for resolving collaborative conflict.	• Introduce tasks that challenge students mathematically and conceptually and provoke mathematical curiosity. • Elicit student thinking. • Listen for students' mathematical intent and name their work to legitimize their ideas and approaches. • Support students to hold the mathematical authority to resolve ambiguity.

FIGURE 4.1   Goals for Phase 3: Building and Sharing Authority

Interactions with the Environment

With your physical environment now designed to allow students to move and obtain what they need freely, you can turn your attention to supporting students to make decisions about what tools and materials they need during collaborative problem-solving. As your students' needs in their environment evolve, keep the following goal in mind:

- Support students to choose tools, materials, and strategies that could work for them in the moment.

Research Note The Relationship Among Students' Authority, Mathematical Learning, and Identity. Being able to in part lead the mathematical work and make decisions about how to work as a group—forms of authority—are important to both learning mathematics and developing a positive identity as a learner and doer of mathematics (Langer-Osuna 2018). Holding authority orients students toward learning opportunities such as sensemaking, communicating one's thinking, or inventing a strategy to solve a problem. Langer-Osuna (2018) argues that, in addition to fostering important learning opportunities, when students hold such authority, they experience themselves—and, importantly, are experienced by others—as mathematical contributors and sense makers. These experiences are the building blocks of a positive mathematics identity.

Support students to choose tools, materials, and strategies that could work for them in the moment.

As students gain familiarity with the tools available and confront new mathematical work, they must learn (and keep learning) how to choose tools to model and represent mathematical concepts. Giving students the authority to choose materials, tools, and strategies means helping them learn to choose. Early on, you'll want to manage the choice somewhat by providing a limited set of material choices that could be supportive. For example, if your students were exploring joining and separating situations, you might provide linking cubes, base ten blocks, and square tiles, which could readily be used to model and solve these problems, but not geoboards or pattern blocks, which would be far more difficult to apply in these problem-solving situations. Providing a set of choices, however, does not preclude you from letting students use other materials in creative ways should they have a plan. Students might, for example, develop an innovative way of using coins to model joining and separating situations that have nothing to do with money, drawing on ideas about place value or skip counting. In such a case, you might simply ask, "How could you use that tool to help you?" and students may very well surprise you.

Students will likely need support to reflect on the utility of available tools. If students struggle to choose a tool or manipulative, you can ask questions to help them think through the decision-making process, such as "What tool could help you see what is happening in this problem?" If students have made a selection that either they are struggling to use or you are struggling to understand, help them step back to think aloud about that choice, with questions like "What are you trying?" and "How could this tool help you?" You can also discuss with the whole class what tools students chose and how helpful different tools were for different groups. Remember that students do not need to be successful in using each tool they select; in fact, recognizing when a manipulative is *not* working is a sign of meaningful learning. And also remember that the tools students choose are deeply connected to the strategies they are developing; that is, what tool students use depends on how they might use it. Choosing a tool is part of developing a strategy and therefore part of mathematical learning. Support students to choose, try, and reflect on their choices and to use the structure you have set up in your physical environment to make this process possible.

Interactions with Mathematics

Mathematics is the engine of the goals for collaboration in this phase, and as such we are going to focus on these interactions first, before diving into interactions with others. The kinds of mathematical work students are trying together and how you as their teacher facilitate that work demand and promote collaboration. It all begins with presenting students with the kinds of tasks that press them to do deep thinking. Then, you have a prominent role during collaborative problem-solving to elicit, interpret, recognize, name, and support students' developing mathematical thinking, a process often referred to as *conferring* (Munson 2018). Finally, take advantage of moments when students are actively struggling to maintain their mathematical authority over sensemaking. As you plan to build student authority, keep the following goals in mind:

- Introduce tasks that challenge students mathematically and conceptually and provoke mathematical curiosity.
- Elicit student thinking.
- Listen for students' mathematical intent and name their work to legitimize their ideas and approaches.
- Support students to hold the mathematical authority to resolve ambiguity.

Introduce tasks that challenge students mathematically and conceptually and provoke mathematical curiosity.

Your role is twofold in this goal: to choose rich tasks and to introduce them to students in ways that maintain their richness. In Chapter 2, we discussed what makes a rich task. Then, we were concerned with choosing the first few tasks of the year, with the goal of engaging students so you could observe and set norms. In this phase, the tasks you choose focus on developing students' understanding of math concepts. Rich tasks need to be open, inviting students to participate in many ways, while also *addressing big mathematical ideas* (Boaler, Munson, and Williams 2017–2021) and being *groupworthy* (Cohen and Lotan 2014; Featherstone et al. 2011), two ideas worth digging into.

For tasks to challenge students mathematically and conceptually, they need to focus on big ideas or concepts that take time to develop (often years) and undergird other mathematical ideas. For instance, a rich task could focus on the meaning of area as a big idea, rather than the formula for calculating the area of a rectangle as "length times width," which is just a procedure. There is no fixed set of big ideas in mathematics, but various standards documents (National Governors Association Center for Best Practices and Council of Chief State School Officers 2010; Common Core Standards Writing Team 2013), policies (NCTM 2014), and curricular materials (Boaler, Munson, and Williams 2017–2021; Fosnot 2008) have offered different ways of describing and naming big mathematical ideas. The key is that big ideas require deep understanding, and that understanding supports students in making sense of future mathematical work.

RICH VS. NOT RICH TASKS

Consider these two tasks:

I have 36 crackers to share. If 3 friends share the crackers equally, how many crackers will each friend get?	I have 36 crackers. If I want to share the crackers equally, how many friends can share? How many crackers will each friend get? Find as many ways to share the crackers equally as you can. What patterns do you see? (Boaler, Munson, and Williams 2018)

The task on the left is only open in that students might use a variety of strategies to solve it. It has only one answer, and many students could solve it alone fairly quickly. Because the task is fairly closed, it only touches on a big idea—making equal groups—but does not engage students in developing deep thinking about this idea. Compare this to the task on the right, which has many answers that are systematically related to factor pairs. This task invites students to grapple with making equal groups and, ultimately, the meaning of division and its relationship to multiplication. In this task, students benefit from having a partner to help them generate solutions, model the task, organize their thinking, and look for patterns. The task on the right is a rich task: open, addressing big ideas, and groupworthy.

Meaningful work invites, and even demands, collaboration. Tasks should be groupworthy, which means students need to talk to and work with others. A groupworthy task would be daunting for students as individuals, but with a partner or two, students can generate ideas, try strategies, make sense, ask questions, and struggle productively. You can read more about groupworthy tasks in Featherstone and colleagues' (2011) book *Smarter Together!*

When you introduce a task to students, your role is to maintain the richness of the task (Jackson et al. 2012). Launch the task by making sure students understand the context and what the question is asking, be clear about the resources students have at their disposal (manipulatives, chart paper, partners, etc.), and send them off to work. Resist any temptation to give students hints about how to solve or point them toward particular answers. Research shows that these efforts are counterproductive, reducing the cognitive demand (see Chapter 2), and making the task less rich by turning it into a procedure. For instance, if Mary were introducing the cracker problem (see Rich vs. Not Rich Tasks, page 80), she would read the task, make sure students understood what it meant that the crackers were "shared equally," point out that this task has many solutions and that students were expected to find as many as possible, show students bowls of 36 square tiles they could use to model the task if they wanted, and say that they could also select their own methods. She would not hint that this task was asking "___ × ___ = 36" or phrase it as a series of questions like "If 2 friends shared, how many crackers would they each get? If 3 friends shared, how many crackers would they each get? If 4 friends shared, how many crackers would they each get? . . ." This way of launching the task would reduce it to a set of procedures.

When choosing and launching tasks, you'll want to consider some key questions:

- What big idea do you want students to focus on?
- What tasks can you find that address this big idea?
- Is the task open?
- Is the task groupworthy? Would students benefit from collaborating to work on the task?
- How could you launch the task so that you maintain its richness?

Elicit student thinking.

As students work together on the mathematical tasks you have chosen and introduced, your role is to circulate throughout the classroom, conferring with partners about their developing ideas. Your central role is to elicit student thinking by asking partners questions about the task, how they understand the mathematical work, and/or the strategies they are developing or trying to tackle that work.

How does eliciting student thinking support collaboration? This goal sits at the intersection of interactions with mathematics and with others, because you are simultaneously uncovering how students are making sense of the mathematics and supporting students to share their thinking with one another. For students to interact collaboratively with mathematics, their thinking needs to be public. For students to interact with one another, they need to have tools for sharing ideas. By eliciting student thinking you accomplish several things at once:

- You learn about how students are thinking, gathering formative assessment data that can influence your teaching.
- Partners learn about how each other is thinking.
- Students are challenged to articulate their own processes and ideas, which can generate productive struggle, especially in the midst of problem-solving.
- Ideas become the subject of shared consideration and debate among partners.

Eliciting student thinking is core pedagogical practice, and like any practice, it takes time to develop effective questions that you can ask and students have learned how to answer. So, dive in, ask questions, listen to what students tell you, and ask more questions to follow up and learn more. Your questions help students scaffold their explanations to you and for one another. As you approach a group of collaborating students, you can ask initial eliciting questions such as:

- "What are you thinking?"
- "What are you trying?"
- "Tell me about your work so far."
- "How did you get started?"
- "I see you're (using cubes, making a diagram, drawing a picture, etc.). Tell me what this represents."
- "What is the task asking?"
- "Tell me what's happening in this story."

Follow up to help students build on and clarify their explanations with questions such as:

- "What did you do next? Why?"
- "Why are you trying that?"
- "Where did that idea come from?"
- "How will that help you?"
- "Tell me about this part (point to particular elements of students' work)."

Remember that to support collaboration, no one student should speak for the group, and students should address their answers to you *and* their partners. At times this might mean that you have to specifically prompt students to talk to one another with questions like "Can you explain to your partner what your idea is?" By doing so, you support students to hear and engage with one another's ideas.

Research Notes **The Benefits of Eliciting.** In a study of the ways that teachers interact with collaborating students about their mathematical thinking, Webb and colleagues (Webb et al. 2008; Webb 2009) found that eliciting student thinking by inviting students to share their ideas and then asking follow-up questions to probe that thinking had significant impacts. Groups where teachers pressed students to explain their ideas were more likely to develop complete and accurate mathematical explanations, both in the moment and later in the lesson. Alternatively, when teachers simply issued reminders of expectations, made perfunctory comments, or asked initial questions without probing the details, students were less likely to develop their explanations during the interaction. For eliciting to influence student thinking, teachers must listen to and engage with that thinking by asking questions that support students to explain.

There is much to learn about eliciting and interpreting student thinking. For those who would like to learn more, you can find recommended reading in the appendix.

Listen for students' mathematical intent and name their work to legitimize their ideas and approaches.

When you elicit student thinking, you must listen closely to interpret what students are trying to communicate. Thinking aloud is messy, imprecise, incomplete, and constantly under revision. Students are often sharing first-draft thinking, searching for the words to describe their ideas and trying to order them. Their ideas typically come out in partial sentences, out of order and sometimes circular. We encourage you to focus not on these qualities, but on students' *mathematical intent*. Underneath their attempts is an idea. It may be a mathematical concept, a strategy for solving the problem, a connection to a related task, or a model that could help them make sense of the situation. Students are in the process of inventing ideas for which they do not yet have the words. Your role is to listen for what they mean and help them find the words to describe their ideas. As you listen, consider the following questions:

- What are students doing or trying?
- What concepts are they using or coming to understand?

- What are they struggling to express?
- What words could you use to name their ideas that could help them both learn and communicate?

Revoice what you hear. When you revoice, you check in with a student to ensure that you understood them correctly, position them as the authors of ideas, and, possibly, restate those ideas in more formal or complete mathematical language. For instance, when a pair of Faith's students were trying to determine if the equation $9 = 10 - 1$ was true or false, they built a stick of 9 cubes and had some additional cubes they wanted to use, but struggled to explain how and why. After several eliciting questions, it became clear that the students wanted to represent $10 - 1$ with the other cubes and weren't sure whether to make 10 or 1 or something else. Faith revoiced this strategy with mathematical language, saying, "So you want to represent each side of the equation with these cubes, with these representing 9 and these representing $10 - 1$?" When her first graders agreed, she followed up by asking, "Once you represent both sides of the equation, what will you do?" When her students said, "Put them together," Faith asked if the students meant to combine or compare them, which clarified that they intended to compare the two sticks to see if they were equal lengths. Faith was able to figure out her students' mathematical intent, check her interpretation, name the strategy so that students could explain this idea in the future, and legitimize this approach as mathematically valid. Listen through students' first-draft thinking for their intent to nurture ideas at their earliest stages. Your students have ideas; your role is to learn to see them.

> **Research Note** **Listening to Students' Ideas, Not Just Their Words.** Students often have powerful mathematical ideas that they struggle to communicate effectively or clearly. The work of Judit Moschkovich (1999, 2010) has shown the importance of teachers listening for students' mathematical ideas, rather than focusing on the precision or completeness of their communication, when attending and responding to students' mathematical contributions to classroom discussions. Along with Enyedy and colleagues (2008), Moschkovich found that when teachers revoice students' mathematical ideas, they are able to accept students' thinking, establish students as the authors of the ideas, and return the ideas in more precise or clear language, supporting language development.

Support students to hold the mathematical authority to resolve ambiguity.

During the course of mathematical work, students will very likely come to you with confusions or debates with the expectation that you will resolve the ambiguity, tell them what to do, or serve as the referee declaring who is right. For instance, when Mary's fourth graders were working on a problem involving loading 156 cans of juice into 6 slots inside a vending machine, one group argued about whether this task involved multiplication or division and called Mary over to settle the dispute. Mary resisted, putting the questions back to the group: How *could* this be multiplication? How *could* this be division?

When your students want you to be the mathematical referee, we encourage you to resist this positioning, just as Mary did. Seize the opportunity to keep the mathematical authority with students and help them stay in and move through whatever challenge they face. Students need to be reminded that they are capable of figuring out what ideas make sense; if you step in and do the work for them, you rob them of the opportunity to learn. That said, they may need some support. If students are struggling or want you to save them from their struggles, use some moves to help them name and then think through the struggle without doing the work for them. You might ask:

- "What is making this hard right now?"
- "What is your question? What do you each think about that question?"
- "What choices do you have?"
- "What could you try?"
- "So you disagree. Could you each explain your thinking to me and each other?"
- "Show us what you mean."
- Ask one partner after another has shared an idea: "What do you think about this idea?"

When Mary invited her group to wrestle with how multiplication and division might represent the vending machine task, students were able to articulate some reasons why each might make sense. But they were not able to resolve their dispute. This is, of course, because they were all right; partitioning 156 cans into 6 groups can be thought of as division ($156 \div 6 =$ ___) or multiplication ($6 \times$ ___ $= 156$). But her students were convinced that only one could be correct. Mary knew that at the heart of this debate was a mathematical idea—the relationship between multiplication and division—that all her students could benefit from grappling with. She decided to bring their question to the whole-class discussion, asking all students, "Is this a multiplication or division task? Why? How do you know?"

During whole-class discussion, students' ambiguous language, confusion, or conflicting answers from peers might create opportunities to pose productive mathematical dilemmas. Building on the idea of listening for the mathematics, you might revoice their understanding or confusions to crystallize the dilemma for the class to consider. Then invite the whole class into the debate by asking questions such as "What do you all think about that? Do you all agree/disagree?" In this way, you again affirm students' authority and competence to resolve mathematical confusion and develop new ideas. Refusing to serve as the sole mathematical authority in the room creates rich learning opportunities for all students.

Interactions with Others

In the collaborative classroom, students engage with mathematics and the environment through interactions with others. Interactions with others are at the heart of this work because it is through sharing, making sense of, and building on one another's ideas that learning with understanding occurs. Students also begin to see themselves, and one another, as young mathematicians through interacting with others in a range of important mathematical practices. Therefore, in this phase, you will be supporting students in learning to listen to one another and make sense of one another's thinking, make mathematical decisions together and resolve conflict when they hit upon disagreements. As you plan to build student authority through interactions with others, keep the following goals in mind:

- Establish routines that support students in listening to and making sense of each other.
- Redirect decision-making to partners or peers.
- Build tools for resolving collaborative conflict.

Establish routines that support students in listening to and making sense of each other's thinking.

Children do not necessarily know how to be good mathematical partners to one another. You can establish simple, effective routines that support peers in attending to one another's thinking, listening for and making sense of peers' mathematical ideas, and responding in productive ways. One such routine is peer revoicing. Peer revoicing holds students accountable for attending to and making sense of others' ideas and offers peers a chance to confirm that they are being heard correctly.

Another routine is orchestrating reflective whole-class conversations about what makes for good partnerships, how partnerships went that day, and what students might try the next day to build better partnerships. These conversations make space for students to name and troubleshoot problems, such as when peers ignore them or take control, or there are other obstacles to collaboration.

Both these routines foster two important goals: joint mathematical thinking and mutual recognition as learners and doers of mathematics. Education research and practice has long focused on the importance of thinking together in learning mathematical concepts, but as important—perhaps even more important—is the development of a positive sense of self as a young mathematician. When students are positively oriented to the discipline of mathematics and mathematical activity, learning happens. In this sense, identity is at the core of learning. Routines that support students in recognizing and affirming one another as legitimate mathematical thinkers and doers go a long way in fostering positive mathematical identities.

Other routines beyond revoicing and reflective discussions about productive partnerships can also promote both joint thinking and mutual recognition. For example, routines that support students in coming to a shared understanding of the task help students get on the same page, which enables more productive shared thinking and helps students more easily recognize the contributions of their peers. Similarly, routines that support students with agreeing on a strategy before the group begins also help students build on their early ideas on how to enter the task and come to a common approach.

Once students begin working on the problem together by trying out strategies, support revoicing through language stems such as "So, I heard you say that . . . Is that right?"

Moves that check for agreement, such as "Do you agree?" or "What do you think?," or stems to promote elaboration or clarification of ideas, such as "Can you say more about . . . ?" or "Can you repeat?," support students in being clear about one another's thinking and ensuring that each student is heard and understood.

Redirect decision-making to partners or peers.

Even when you are establishing routines that support students to listen to and make sense of one another's thinking, they may still come to you for approval of their decisions or for you to make decisions for them. They might ask, "What should we do next?" Students may have heard one another's thinking but struggle to make a decision together, or they may have made a decision, but feel insecure about proceeding without your stamp of approval. To reinforce students' mathematical authority, you must gently, but firmly, return these kinds of questions back to partners and stay to help them grapple with possible answers. This does not mean that you simply leave students stuck; instead, stay with them and ask questions that help them engage with one another's ideas and make the decision together, equitably. You could ask:

- "What do you (partner) think about that idea?"
- "Which idea could you try first?"
- "Why does this plan make sense to you?"

In the same vein, students will want to talk to *you* instead of each other when you approach a collaborating group. Don't assume that the student who talks first (or the only student who speaks) represents everyone's thinking. Ask all the partners to share their ideas to unearth disagreements or differences in understanding. And prompt the students to talk to each other instead of just to you. Give specific directions, like "Tell them" or "Show them," when students face and talk only to you. Similarly, questions such as "What do you think of (peer's) idea? Do you agree?" support peers in responding to the contributions of others.

Build tools for resolving collaborative conflict.

Collaboration doesn't just involve mathematical ideas. In fact, to even get to the mathematical ideas, students have to negotiate the relational aspects of working together, including sharing materials and space, taking turns, getting one another's attention, distributing responsibilities, sharing resources, and coming to a shared understanding of what is expected of them within the task. Sometimes students each want control over these decisions, and sometimes they want their partners to do it for them. In either situation, inequities creep in and learning can get stymied. Even when collaborative dynamics are going well, students may also confront mathematical disagreements and might dig their heels on their perspective in ways that are mathematically unproductive.

Students therefore need tools for resolving conflict, both relational and mathematical.

Some routines for how to solve these conflicts can be simple, such as the game of rock-paper-scissors to decide who goes first. Language stems for making a suggestion or request, such as "Can we . . . ?" or "Maybe we can . . . ?," can also promote more productive resolutions to conflict. Routines that help students regularly orient and refer to the class norms can also support conflict resolution by grounding expectations in the classroom community.

Routines that foster mutual recognition, such as revoicing, help students recognize one another's contributions, which also supports conflict resolution over time as students come to trust the mathematical thinking of their peers as well as their own mathematical thinking. Such trust supports students in taking multiple ideas into consideration and grounding mathematical decision-making within the discipline of mathematics itself, rather than in the perceived status of students. In the debrief discussion ask, "What did your partner do today that helped you both move forward?" Or suggest to students, "Thank your partner for something they did today." Questions such as "Did anyone resolve a conflict today? How did you do it?" also support the development of conflict resolution tools within the classroom community and help students take ownership over their partnerships.

Rollout

As in the previous phase, the eight goals described in this chapter are not a checklist; instead, building students' capacity to navigate interactions with the environment, others, and mathematics requires pushing multiple goals forward simultaneously. In this section, we describe how Faith and Mary roll out these eight goals in their classrooms. We have segmented this phase into two loose stages and labeled them each by weeks for ease, but the amount of time Faith and Mary spend varies depending on their students. Similarly, we have begun with weeks 1 to 3 to indicate whenever you begin this phase of mathematics work, regardless of the point in your school calendar when this occurs.

Because they are different teachers and they teach different grades, their rollout plans have some things in common and some key differences. Each of the stages begins with describing both teachers' shared goals and how they approach making progress toward them. Then, Mary and Faith each describe the work they do with students that is distinct, including routines on which they focus, what they pay attention to and for, and the types of discussions and interactions they foster.

Weeks 1–3+: Teaching Students Collaborative Routines and Tools

As we begin to roll out the goals in this phase, you'll notice a focus first on interactions with others. Students need routines and tools to use to get started on and move through collaborative mathematical work. A central focus in these weeks for Mary and Faith is introducing, practicing, and reflecting on some key routines and tools and then slowly layering in new ones as the need arises and students are ready. In this part of the rollout, students need a revoicing routine to orient to one another's thinking and a quick conflict resolution routine like rock-paper-scissors or referring to the class norms.

As you work on your current juicy mathematical unit, carefully choosing tasks worthy of collaboration, thread in days where the focus of the launch is teaching students new tools and practicing them, as in a fishbowl or through turning and talking with a partner. You can do this when a task or game continues from one day to the next and students only need reminding of the task. Then you can spend time in the launch focusing on *how* we work together. In fact, you can make the revoicing routine a part of a math game so that to do the task, students must revoice. Similarly, you can make deciding how to begin or revoicing the task a part of the launch so that students get practice solving or preempting conflict with the tools you give them.

First Grade: FAITH

I begin with the end in mind: authentic and joyful collaboration, students holding mathematical authority, and thoughtfully choosing tools, strategies, and materials to support their learning. Work toward these goals begins and is sustained by language-centered routines that I introduce and students practice until they become habits. That way, as new challenges arise, these talk routines act as an anchor, a familiar tool to support conflict resolution, wrestling with ambiguity, or agreeing on a next step.

These language routines can be as simple as saying "Maybe we can . . . ?" as partners make decisions or arrive at a disagreement, something I described in Chapter 3. Through repeated practice, nudges and prompts in partnership conferences, and students sharing stories in our closing circles about how they used "Maybe we can . . . ?" in their work together, not only does the sentence starter become a habit, we also center collaboration, mutual decision-making, and expressing interest in your partner's thoughts, feelings, and ideas through different stages of their shared work.

Introducing, modeling, and practicing a revoicing routine is similarly critical. As I observed in Jose and Joanna's partnership, this routine must be taught, attended to, and practiced as explicitly as we teach the directions of a math game, or the steps of a task. We practice asking questions to our partner: "How many dots do you see?" or "What combination of 10 did you make?" We practice answering these questions: "I think . . ." or "I saw . . ." We practice prompting our partner to explain by asking, "How do you know?" We practice explaining, "I know because . . ." We practice revoicing this explanation to affirm what was shared and make sure we understood what our partner did and said: "So I heard you say . . . Is that right?" Finally, we practice either saying "Yes, do you agree?" or "No, that's not right" and explaining it a different way.

This routine does so much for students: primes them for listening intently, encourages active sensemaking, highlights the value of each person's contributions, and builds student authority. We practice this routine in our morning meeting as we share about our weekend or something exciting we learned. I model and we practice this routine in all kinds of conversations with students at their tables during breakfast. For example, one morning, in the weeks leading up to Halloween, a table of students were giving hints and guessing each other's Halloween costumes. I kneeled by their table, smiling and listening in. Luis gave his clue: "I'm going to be a superhero who fights crime at night!"

Eva quickly called out, "Ooh, I think you're going to be Batman!"

I turned to her and asked, "How do you know?"

She talked about the clues, particularly the part about fighting crime at night, and said she knows that Batman comes out at night, like bats do. I modeled revoicing what she said, to make sure we all understood what she was saying, which she happily affirmed, and then we all turned to Luis to see if she was right (she was). We practice, and model, and nudge each other and celebrate until it becomes a habit, not just to revoice each other's thinking, but to care for and actively listen to what they're saying.

Fourth Grade: MARY

I set up routines in my room that will support students in beginning to explore having authority over their decision-making. These routines and structures allow students to reflect on how things are going, whether they are successful or still grappling. The goal is for students to begin to see that they can make decisions for themselves and repair or rethink those decisions when they lead to harm or unsuccessful work.

In the launch, I introduce three guiding questions that support students to negotiate how they will engage in the work of the day.

1. "Should we work on the same strategy or work side by side?" At this point in the year, we have done enough reflective work that students should know their preference. This question prompts students to negotiate their own needs and preferences as a mathematician while also engaging in collaborative work.

2. "What strategy are you/we going to use?" This prompts a conversation about how students will engage in the mathematical work and supports students that might be grappling with where to begin. It also helps students articulate their strategy before launching into the problem-solving work.

3. "Do you need more alone time to think or are you ready to get started?" This orients students to being reflective about their understanding of the task and their strategy and dismantles the idea that needing more think time means that you are less of a mathematician.

We do this routine every day in the launch. Students turn and talk to discuss each question to allow time for them to make sense of their work together and share what they need as mathematicians. Sometimes what one person needs is in direct conflict with what another person needs, and students need support with deciding how to proceed collaboratively. At this point in the year, students grapple with negotiating their needs and the needs of their partner. But this grappling will support them to gain the skills they need to productively work with a partner.

While they are discussing their strategy with a partner, they also discuss what manipulatives might be useful. This conversation also leads students to negotiate whether they want to work on a shared product (shared manipulatives or on one piece of paper) or if they want to have their own work. During this phase, students rarely decide to have one product because they are used to working independently.

I invite students that need more time or support with this work to stay at the carpet longer. I am careful to not facilitate the conversation, but I sit with them until they have come to a decision or I feel like they have the skills to work it out together. For example, one day a partnership was really grappling with which strategy to use. When I dismissed the rest of the class, we sat there in silence with the students facing me until I prompted them to have a conversation about how to proceed. I said, "This is your time to figure out what to do. How should our bodies look when we are having a conversation?"

Students responded, "Facing each other and giving eye contact."

To which I replied, "Yes, I am here as a support, but you two are the mathematicians that need to decide which strategy to use. I don't have the answer. I will sit here with you while you figure it out, but I will just be listening."

Once they were facing each other and started discussing, I sat there looking around the room and seemingly not paying attention to their conversation, to shift the authority from me to them. But I was still there in case they needed support.

Weeks 3 and Beyond: Building Collaboration Using the Lesson Structure

Once students have learned and practiced routines that help them engage in collaborative mathematical work, you can shift your focus to maintaining and deepening their understandings and skills. Rather than regular intensive practice, you might shift to weekly or, eventually, even less frequent reflective discussions where students revisit these practices and discuss how things are going. Inevitably, routines or talk moves that you have practiced with the class will periodically need to be reinforced with specific partnerships or the whole class. Meanwhile, goals related to interactions with mathematics and the environment become more prominent, as you use the lesson structure to focus on supporting student thinking and decision-making.

You might stay in this phase the entire rest of the year. This is complex work for both you and students and can take time, depending on your and your students' prior experience with collaboration. Building and working in a collaborative mathematics classroom is ongoing, daily work that we don't accomplish and check off the list. In this part of the rollout, Mary and Faith leverage their launch-explore-discuss lesson structure to do different kinds of work toward their goals. In the following sections, we describe how you can use these different parts of your lesson to reinforce, extend, or move toward your goals of building and sharing authority.

During the Launch

The launch is a useful time to set the tone for the day, proactively introduce something new, practice a routine that needs refreshing, or create space for students to get off on the right foot. Depending on what needs you have assessed in your community, you might use the launch to:

- Practice a routine like negotiating turn taking or revoicing one another's thinking. This practice can stand alone or you can embed it in a game or task for the day. Students can also practice routines like revoicing in whole-class discussions like number talks.
- Address a trend you noticed on a previous day: a challenge like partners ignoring one another's ideas, or a success like a new productive talk move you observed in a partnership that others could benefit from.
- Give space for partnering students to make initial decisions together, like where to sit, what materials to get, and who will take on different leadership roles. This gives you the opportunity to listen in on and respond to the ways that students are negotiating decisions with one another. You can also highlight language students use that is equitable and supports joint decision-making.
- Continue to introduce tasks that foster collaboration and mathematical curiosity.

During Collaborative Group Work

Collaborative work time is, of course, where the rubber meets the road. You are asking students to be collaborative and put into action all the tools, strategies, and routines you have taught them, and they will undoubtedly do so in many different ways. Similarly, this is the time when you focus on both students' collaboration and their mathematical ideas. Every day, use collaborative work time to:

- Elicit student thinking and support students to articulate how they are making sense together of the mathematics. (See Munson 2018 for more on this process.)
- Look for opportunities where there is ambiguity to hold students accountable for making sense with one another. Resist making decisions for students.
- Listen for both mathematical ideas and collaborative moves that you can share with the class in the whole-class discussion. For example, Mary once noticed a pair of students working together in the same notebook, something that was new for that class. She invited them to share their new strategy and the reasons for it with the whole class.
- Redirect student questions and challenges to partners to support joint authority.

- Listen for collaborative challenges and help scaffold interactions within partnerships so that students can resolve these challenges equitably.
- Support students to make decisions together.
- Assess whether students need to revisit routines or add new ones to address their collaborative challenges. These can then be taught or practiced in the launch in upcoming days.

During the Discussion

Although the discussion is intended to foreground students' mathematical work, you can still use this time to address and build on students' collaborative efforts. You might use the discussion to:

- Invite students to reflect on their partnerships. You can ask: "Who had a partnership that felt productive today? What did your partner do to make your work go well (or to listen to your thinking or help you both make decisions)?" This discussion should be asset focused like Mary's was in the opening of this chapter.
- Share collaborative moves that you noticed when talking with partnerships that you'd like others to try.

First Grade: FAITH

I leverage the transition from the launch to explore to model, remind, and practice the routine of getting set up to work collaboratively, so that more of our explore time can be spent growing mathematical collaboration. Negotiating and agreeing on routines like choosing a good place to work, choosing and getting our materials, or deciding who goes first are critical steps but can also consume most of the explore time, especially if disagreements or confusions arise.

To combat this, especially if it's something I observed during work time the previous day, I close the launch by first making sure all students understand the task ahead, then gesturing to our anchor chart that reminds us how partners get set up to work collaboratively. I ask if a partnership can model getting started. As Riham and Jimena get up off the rug, I begin narrating out loud. "Notice how Riham and Jimena are coming together. I am noticing that they are first deciding where the best spot to work is. I just heard Riham ask Jimena, 'Maybe we can work in the library.' Oh, now I am noticing that Riham is getting the materials for the game, and Jimena is getting paper and something to write with. Mathematicians, do you notice how they have made a plan for how to get started and are quickly getting the things that they need? Do you notice how they are checking in with each other by asking questions, and saying 'Maybe we can'? Oh, now I am seeing they are sitting side by side and have put their materials in the middle, and now they are doing rock-paper-scissors to see who gets to roll the dice first. There they go!"

I turn my attention back to the children on the rug. "Mathematicians, did you notice how Riham and Jimena got to work quickly by making suggestions, deciding on a plan, and making sure they both agree? Thumbs up if you and your partner can get started just like Riham and Jimena did!" As partnerships are invited to get started, I do more abbreviated voice-overs for the second partnership, and then the third partnership, and soon all students are off the rug, and we settle into the buzz and busyness of the explore part of our math block.

Giving these reminders before the collaborative work begins, and providing repeated voice-overs with students modeling, streamlines the work of setting up for collaboration, freeing us all up to be curious and challenged by the math task at hand.

Fourth Grade: MARY

I see the link between the discussion and the launch that follows the next day as exceptionally important. During the discussion, students reflect on the successes and challenges that arose, and the launch is where I remind students of the ideas they developed the day before. The first question in the discussion is "How did your partnerships go today?" My goal is for students to name something, even if it's just one thing, to bring back in the launch the next day to support students in trying on a skill or habit. The two elements work together to support students to be reflective about their work, identifying one thing that they can try on the next day and then the space to revisit the habit before the explore. For example, in a discussion one day in early October, I asked, "How did your partnerships go?" and a student responded with "We were working side by side on different strategies, but my strategy was taking a long time and I got mad, so I decided to try my partner's strategy. I think I got a little confused about how Angela used her strategy, but I wasn't mad anymore." This student did two things that I wanted to highlight in the launch the next day. She changed her strategy when it wasn't efficient and she tried her partner's strategy. These are two habits of a mathematician that will support the collaborative work and the mathematics. For the launch the next day, I highlighted this and asked "What could she have done to make sure she understood Angela's strategy?" Students need a lot of support with how to utilize conversation to support their thinking.

Questions to Consider as You Plan Your Rollout

Here are a few questions you might think through as you map your own way to roll out the goals in this phase.

- What have I learned about my students already as collaborators?

  - ▶ What can they negotiate fairly?
  - ▶ What do they struggle to negotiate at this point?
  - ▶ What kinds of collaborative conflicts are frequent?
  - ▶ What kinds of supports might they need to build negotiations?

- What collaborative routines have they learned? What routines are still wobbly?
- What collaborative routines or talk moves from this chapter do you want your students to learn?
- What student partnerships seem productive?

  - ▶ What makes them productive?
  - ▶ What are these students doing that others could learn from to be more productive in their partnerships?

- How are students explaining their thinking? What eliciting support do they need from you to share their ideas?
- What kinds of tasks seem to promote collaboration in your classroom?

  - ▶ Where did these come from?
  - ▶ What are the features of these tasks that seem to support collaboration and learning?
  - ▶ How could you adapt other tasks to include those features?

Reflecting Along the Way

As you roll out these goals with your students, pay close attention to how things are going, their developing capacities to collaborate for mathematical work, and what they may be struggling with. We've found these reflection questions to be useful tools, and they can also support reflective conversations with your colleagues as you co-plan or learn together.

Reflecting on Interactions with the Environment

● Are students regularly choosing materials and strategies that support sensemaking and shared thinking?

  ○ Are there any materials students need access to but don't have?
  ○ Are there any materials that seem to be distracting or derailing students?
  ○ How could I support students in making these decisions together?

Reflecting on Interactions with Others

● What collaborative conflicts keep surfacing?

  ○ Are students able to move through these conflicts without your intervention?
  ○ If not, what routines could you introduce to help students address these conflicts? Or, are there routines you could revisit in the launch or discussion?

● Do students want you to resolve their conflicts?

  ○ How can you redirect these conflicts to the partnership?
  ○ How can you stay with students to resolve the conflict without doing it for them?

● Are students listening to one another's ideas?

  ○ How can you tell?
  ○ How can you build revoicing into routines, tasks, or games?
  ○ Are students sharing their ideas with one another?
  ○ Are students leaving anyone out of the reasoning?

Reflecting on Interactions with Mathematics

- Are students struggling productively together with the mathematics?

  - How do you know?
  - Are students able to move through struggle to new ideas?
  - When students disagree about the mathematics, what do they do?

- Are you able to get students to share their thinking with you and each other?

  - What eliciting moves seem to help most often?
  - When do students struggle to explain?
  - What opportunities to practice might they need? What language might they need?
  - What ideas are they coming up with that they don't have names for yet?

If . . . Then . . .

In this section we offer some thoughts on common questions that arise during this phase of building and sharing authority with students. These suggestions are meant to be utilized as classroom routines throughout the year.

If students want you to resolve conflict for them, then . . .

Support students' authority to solve their own problems by coaching them to describe the conflict and generate solutions. Revoice what you hear students saying to you and press them to discuss the conflict with each other, rather than refereeing the dispute. For instance, if one partner is controlling the manipulatives when the other wants access, you might repeat what you heard the students say: "So you're saying, Jorge, that you want to use the linking cubes to model the problem, but Sara is not letting you use the cubes. Is that right?" Revoicing helps name the issue, often elicits more conversation, and models how we should all listen to each other. You might coach students in talking to each other. In this case, you could say, "Jorge, why don't you ask Sara and let's see what she says. Sara, what did you hear Jorge ask?" You might also invite the students to generate solutions by asking, "What could we do?," as in "What could we do so that you both can use the cubes?" Students might benefit from language like "Maybe we can . . ." for suggesting solutions, rather than making demands.

Also, look for assets across your community that you can use as a model. For instance, you might invite Jorge and Sara to look around the classroom to see how other groups are handling this. They might notice that other partnerships have placed the materials between them or that they are taking turns in some way. Looking to their peers as potential models is yet another resource students could use for solving conflict in the future without your assistance.

If a routine that students learned begins to get sloppy, then . . .

Use the launch of a lesson to revisit, reteach, and practice the routine. Hold students accountable for using the routines you have established, while expecting that routines need reinforcement from time to time, especially at transition points, like after school breaks or in new units (see Chapter 6 for more on maintaining your community). For instance, if students learned to revoice one another's thinking when making problem-solving decisions, but have been listening to one another less recently, bring this issue to students' attention during the launch of the next lesson. Regardless of the task, take the opportunity to practice revoicing by asking partners to turn and talk about one way they could get started on the task and then ask the other partner to practice revoicing. You might ask, "What does it feel like when someone revoices your thinking? What does it tell you?" You might tell students that you expect to hear them revoicing one another's suggestions or ideas and remind them how this helps them consider all ideas and make the best decisions as a group. The need to revisit routines in the collaborative math classroom is normal and expected. Make the time to shore up your investment in these routines periodically throughout the year.

If one student takes over problem-solving, excluding partners, then . . .

Pause the group's problem-solving and draw attention to the lack of balance. You may be able to see one student taking over from across the room, with materials all positioned in front of one child who also controls the paper and pencil. Or you may have asked students about their work only to hear from one student, while the others seem bewildered or disengaged. In either case, notice aloud the unequal distribution of power and control. You might say, "It looks like you have all the materials" or "It sounds like your group doesn't understand (or agree with) your approach." Remind students that they are expected to do joint work, not just find an answer, and hold the student who has taken over accountable by saying something like "You need to allow your partners to contribute." You might need to have the student who has taken over explain what they are doing until the partners both understand and agree or support the group in renegotiating the problem-solving strategy altogether. Do not allow the group to restart work on the task until they agree on an approach and each member has a way to contribute.

If this inequity is pervasive in your classroom, then it can be a sign that students have not internalized what it means to do joint work. The class as a whole may need to see more models for what it means to work together, and students may need you to reiterate that if only one person finds an answer—even if it is correct—but the other partners were left out, they have not met your expectations for mathematical work.

If students can't agree on materials or strategies, then . . .

At times, all students need is a simple solution for negotiating, such as agreeing to try both approaches and only choosing which one to try first. The two approaches can serve to make mathematical connections and check one another. If students are just bickering, you can prompt them to figure out a path forward by asking, "How are we going to decide?"

But sometimes, particularly when this conflict comes up repeatedly in a partnership, it might mean that these students truly need different models or strategies for making sense of the mathematics. If that is the case, then these students might not be well matched as partners. For instance, if one student wants to model a multidigit separating task with cubes, counting each one, while the other partner wants to decompose the numbers using place value and model the task on an open number line, then these two students are in very different places in their developing conceptual understanding. It would be counterproductive to ask either to give up their approach; instead, they may each need a partner who can make sense of their chosen approach. Choosing a productive partner is, in part, about finding someone who is in a conceptually similar place, who likes similar models or tools, and who understands the same strategies. You may need to help students adjust their partnerships by walking with them around the room looking for other students using cubes or open number lines, for instance.

If students finish fast, then . . .

It is likely the task was either not challenging or open-ended enough to sustain students' productive struggle or collaboration. Choosing or creating the right kind of task is a prerequisite to meaningful collaborative work. If all or nearly all your students legitimately finished quickly, then the task was too limited and did not offer opportunities for extended exploration. This could be because there was only one correct answer, or the task did not demand that students develop new conceptual understanding. For instance, Faith plays a true-or-false game with her first graders to help them build understanding of the equal sign. When she poses a problem like $10 - 1 = 9$ and asks, "True or false?," the demand is low, the answer is straightforward, and her students are not grappling with new concepts, because $10 - 1 = 9$ looks like equations they are familiar with. But when she poses the same question with the equation $8 + 2 = 10 - 5$ and others like it, students suddenly have a lot more to debate, model, and discuss, all related back to the big idea of equivalence.

If a small number of students legitimately finished quickly, then they needed a task with a higher ceiling or an extension that they could grapple with. For instance, in our previous example, Faith could ask students who appear to be moving fluidly through complex equations determining "True or false?" to create their own set of true-or-false equations they could swap with others. Creating true-or-false equations is more challenging than evaluating equations and could be a natural extension for those who are ready.

If students struggle to revoice, then . . .

Scaffold revoicing with repeated attempts, and introduce talk moves that can help students listen to and make sense of one another's thinking, such as "Can you repeat that?" In a whole-class discussion setting, hold students accountable for revoicing by asking multiple students to revoice something that one student has shared with the class. You might have someone revoice just the first thing they heard another student say, and then ask other students to add on, so that the class collectively revoices. When students are working collaboratively, you can scaffold by asking one partner to share the beginning of their thinking, followed by the other partners revoicing, before returning to the sharer for the next part of the explanation. Chunking students' ideas into steps or stages can help others listen and understand multistep or multipart ideas.

However, your goal is that students can do this work on their own, and to do so, they will need some talk moves they can use to get clarification when they are struggling. Faith introduces the talk move "Can you repeat that?" that her students can use anytime they feel like they cannot remember or adequately describe what their partner said. Students may also need moves like "What do you mean by . . . ?" if they heard, but did not understand, what their partner said. Talk moves to clarify or hear an explanation again are useful not just to the revoicing student; the sharing student also develops what we think of as second- and third-draft explanations, which get more concise and precise with each repetition, pushing the group's work forward in the process.

If students are off-task, then . . .

Slow down and assess what is going on. As Jenny and Jen have found in their research, off-task does not always, or even most often, mean that students are not meaningfully advancing their partnerships. If students are off task but they are interacting with one another and their off-task talk lasts only briefly (for instance, less than one minute), then most likely these interactions are *supporting* collaboration. Students use brief off-task conversations in surprisingly sophisticated ways: to get into mathematical work, to rebalance power in the group, and to gain access to materials and resources. If what you see are brief off-task interactions, then the best action is to do nothing.

However, if the off-task talk is sustained (for instance, for several minutes) or what is really happening is that students are not collaborating at all but working in parallel, then you need to intervene. Intervene honestly, and with curiosity, rather than catching students misbehaving. Ask questions like "What are you working on?" or "What are you trying?" It could be that students are legitimately finished and need an extension, or that they do not know how to collaborate with one another, or that they had a disagreement that needs repair. Often, students may be off task for extended periods when they do not understand the task they have been asked to engage in. All these possible explanations offer opportunities for you to teach students something useful for the future.

Signs to Celebrate

Celebrating progress toward your goals is critical for your community to grow. Recognize small steps that accumulate into the community you and students are striving for together, just as Mary used reflection at the opening of the chapter to focus the students' attention on what they can and have done to create productive partnerships. The list of signs to celebrate at this, or any, stage is endless, but we'd like to draw your attention to a few signals that you might see that indicate your collaborative classroom is under construction:

1. Students are having collaborative conflicts that they resolve themselves.
2. Students are struggling productively with mathematics ideas, concepts, and tasks.
3. Students can explain their ideas to one another and you.
4. You have identified some questions that elicit student thinking and help students explain reasoning.
5. You have a clear sense of what students understand and what they are struggling with mathematically.
6. Students can revoice one another's thinking.
7. Students are choosing materials and strategies that make sense.
8. Students are making some decisions together regularly, like where to sit and how to get started.
9. Students talk more to each other than to you.
10. Students can transition between whole-class and small-group work seamlessly.

5

Becoming a Student-Led Mathematics Community

Notes from the Classroom

FAITH: Organizing and Counting During Breakfast and Beyond

One of the first tasks in our unit on place value involved doing a classroom inventory: counting classroom items so we'd always know how many of each thing we had and we'd have a quicker way to check and see if anything was missing. I prepared bins with varying quantities of objects, so that partners could decide what kind of task they wanted to take on. Maybe they wanted to count many different things in smaller quantities, or maybe they would spend two math blocks counting all our linking cubes. I launched the task by presenting our very real-world problem of having so many things and often being unsure or frustrated by not knowing what we actually had. "Like the pens!" one student said. "You say there should always be enough for everyone but then sometimes there isn't, and we don't know until we all need one for writing time!" There was universal excitement as we dove into the work. Ayda and Sara counted all our Elephant and Piggy books, and Angela and Roger counted all our colored pencils, finding that bundling them in tens using rubber bands made it really quick to recount and check their work. The next morning during breakfast, I was preparing the poster paper for our number talk when Ufiata and Theresa approached me. They'd finished their food and asked if they could keep counting and organizing and making labels for all our tools and supplies. I noticed other students listen in and perk up as they heard this idea. I asked them to propose this idea to the whole class, taking a minute to rehearse what they would say. What I had planned as a two-day task to introduce place value became a collective and joyful responsibility. We established a small area where active organizing projects could live, and bundling of items in groups of ten (which we established over time was really helpful with large quantities) and counting and recounting quickly felt important and exciting. Some students even began offering their organizing services to other classrooms, and I was so proud to follow their spark.

MARY: "Could We Use This for Math?"

During a science lesson, we watched a video that asked students to estimate how many bones we have in our bodies. After discussing our estimates, I projected a table that showed the number of bones by location in the body. We talked about how accurate our estimates were and students shared their shock about the quantity. Then something amazing happened. A student raised her hand and said, "Wait, this table looks like a math problem. Could we use this for math?" It was early spring and we had already done several units where students engaged in addition and subtraction work. We were in the midst of fractions and I didn't really want to derail their progress, but I was also excited. This was the moment I had been waiting for all year. My students had shifted their mindsets about math. They were mathematizing outside of our math work times, they could see mathematical situations, and they were excited to solve mathematical problems.

I decided this was a request I couldn't turn down, so I replied, "What does everyone else think? Should we use this table to solve math problems tomorrow?" Most students nodded or gave excited exclamations. The next day, we discussed their math questions about the table, and they went off to solve their inquiries. It wasn't a task where the cognitive demand was high, but I wanted their inquiry and curiosity to be validated. I wanted students to feel like they were in charge of their learning. Allowing them to ask questions and follow their interest was valuable. It was a day to be proud of their progress and of the hard work they had done all year to shift their mindsets.

There's a central paradox to this work: we want students to have authority, but at the same time, this authority is being shared not just with one student, but with a classroom full of students who must learn to share authority with one another. As students begin to take on authority for themselves, how do they decide together what to do and how to think together about solving math problems?

As students navigate collaborative mathematics learning activities, they must learn to share authority with their peers. By sharing authority we mean that students learn to negotiate participation and influence; they take turns, share resources, and take others' ideas into consideration as they make sense of problems and work through them. Without learning to share authority, students' collaborative dynamics can become unbalanced, with some peers dominating the activity, while others are relatively marginalized. Deep learning occurs in dialogue, and unbalanced dynamics prevent dialogue from emerging. Unbalanced dynamics also mean that some students are unable to access important learning opportunities, such as explaining their thinking (Wood 2013), and that other students gain undue influence, spreading mathematical errors that are left unchecked because of issues of status (Langer-Osuna 2016).

As students develop their capacity to build and share authority, they become cocreators of the classroom vision. We can expect to encounter moments when students have ideas for how to adapt the work, norms, and environment to work better for them, and we need to take these ideas seriously in community with students.

In this chapter, we will offer routines for supporting students in sharing authority with one another to foster inclusive and robust collaboration through inquiry and dialogue. We will offer guidance on how to recognize and take advantage of opportunities for students to reshape or renegotiate the work of your collaborative classroom as part of community building. We will also unpack the intersection between the goals of this phase and valued mathematical practices, such as argumentation, justification, and questioning.

Goals for Sharing Authority

In this phase, students begin to orient their voices and their sensemaking toward one another's thinking, in addition to their own, while using and sharing resources (see Figure 5.1). As students learn to share, debate, and connect ideas, the mathematical work deepens and opportunities for rich conceptual understanding—the aha moments—emerge.

Goals for Interactions With . . .		
Environment	**Others**	**Mathematics**
PHASE 4 Becoming a Student-Led Mathematics Community • Give students the tools to notice and the authority to suggest modifications to the classroom environment so it works better for everyone.	• Build tools for co-constructing your work and thinking. • Build tools for resolving mathematical conflict.	• Invite or seize opportunities for students to pose mathematical questions that the class could investigate. • Support mathematical argumentation and discussions.

FIGURE 5.1 Goals for Phase 4: Becoming a Student-Led Mathematics Community

Interactions with the Environment

Goals for interacting with the environment now focus on cocreating a space that serves everyone. Rather than expecting the teacher to single-handedly solve this ambitious problem, in the collaborative classroom we invite students to raise challenges and create possible adjustments. As the teacher, your role is to facilitate these conversations, take student concerns into consideration, and help develop or refine adjustments that are realistic and have potential to improve the learning community.

As you plan to build shared student authority, keep the following goal in mind:

- Give students the tools to notice and the authority to suggest modifications to the classroom environment so it works better for everyone.

Give students the tools to notice and the authority to suggest modifications to the classroom environment so that it works better for everyone.

Communities that foster a sense of belonging allow their members to take on a sense of ownership, or stewardship, of the community itself. This includes having the authority to suggest changes to the environment and invite dialogue with others about such changes. Consider the following issues that students might bring up:

- ■ "It's too noisy in the classroom for us to concentrate. I'm getting overstimulated. Can we have a quiet nook for working with a partner?"
- ■ "There's often a traffic jam getting manipulatives. Can we put together caddies of tools that live on the tables (or our table)?"
- ■ "Everyone wants the cushions in the corner. Can we make another cushion corner? Or draw sticks for turns?"

As a teacher, you might facilitate the class in a discussion of the issue and possible solutions. You might ask, "Do we agree this is an issue?" What one student suggests may only be one possible solution. Ask students, "What else could we do to address this issue?" as students work to come to consensus. The work of coming to a consensus about solving these everyday problems helps students as they begin to engage in mathematical argumentation, where they have to convince each other of their mathematical ideas and solutions.

If there is enough agreement on the issue and the possible solution(s), support students in a trial run. You might suggest, "Let's try that for a week and see how it goes." After a week, facilitate a reflective discussion on how the modification worked. The class might decide to adopt the change, or students might try other solutions and see which one they prefer before deciding. Engaging students in this process, and thereby allowing them to experience actively sharing and building their community, is as important, if not more so, than the actual changes that might genuinely promote greater productivity and joy for your students. These kinds of conversations can happen in math class itself, but they can also occur in morning meeting or closing circle or other times in the day meant for reflection and community.

Interactions with Others

Learning communities offer robust learning experiences when they foster genuine dialogue among their members, including young children. Interactions that foster dialogue are made up of the following kinds of talk moves: (a) eliciting peers' ideas, (b) making sense of peers' thinking, (c) responding to peers productively, and (d) resolving conflict, as needed. These moves depend on successfully gaining peers' attention and orienting peers toward one another as if their ideas are worthy of taking into consideration. How might you support such moves?

As you build a community of learners with your students, it is important to support student interactions directed toward one another, rather than primarily toward you. Students get better at attending to one another and voicing their own ideas, including their strategies, struggles, questions, and curiosities, and others take these contributions seriously. Students learn to build on one another's ideas by making connections or expressing respectful disagreement. Through productive and inclusive interactions with others, students engage with meaningful mathematics learning opportunities in community without getting stuck in unresolved conflict or miscommunication.

As you plan to build a shared mathematics learning community among your students, you will want to keep the following goals in mind:

- Build tools for co-constructing your work and thinking.
- Build tools for resolving mathematical conflict.

Build tools for co-constructing your work and thinking.

Language is an important tool to navigate thinking and learning with others. For example, when students ask questions such as "What could we try?," "What (manipulatives) do you want to use?," or "How did you do it?," they are eliciting ideas from their peers. Talk moves like these foster joint thinking and decision-making.

To build on one another's ideas, students must make sense of each other's thinking. Revoicing routines, as well as asking students to repeat or to show their ideas, helps to ensure that students understand each other's thinking. As a community, support your students in practicing the following moves:

- Revoice/check in: "I hear you say . . . is that right?"
- Ask to repeat if unclear: "Can you repeat what you just said?" "Can you show me what you mean?"

Tools that make thinking visible and public, such as charts, posters, or models that record partners' mathematical strategies side by side or that represent ideas that both partners agreed with, also support making sense of others' thinking.

Once students are able to elicit peers' ideas and make sense of what they are saying, they must also learn to respond to those ideas. Students might respond by agreeing, disagreeing, or adding on to an idea. As a community, support your students in practicing the following moves:

- Express agreement or disagreement respectfully and with explanation/ justification: "I disagree because . . ."

- Add on to ideas or plans: "Yeah, and then we can . . ."
- Make a suggestion about what to do next: "What if we . . . ?"

Have students model, rehearse, and practice talk moves and interactional routines such as revoicing. You might use a fishbowl (see Chapter 3, page 51). You might also show students artifacts that illustrate shared thinking and ask students to narrate how they built them together. Then reflect with students on how these interactions served the collaboration and what they might try the next time they engage in mathematical work together.

As you prepare to facilitate such reflection discussions, listen, during small-group conferences, for students who are already building on one another's ideas and negotiating the work together. By using this asset-focused approach, you support students in noticing and naming productive interactions. Consider filming students during productive moments and showing the video to the class and asking, "How did they build ideas together?" This allows students to build a bank of productive interactional routines and ways of talking to one another that arises from within their own classroom community.

Build tools for resolving mathematical conflict.

Even in the most productive communities, conflict is inevitable. Humans come together with different ideas, preferences, and understandings and must navigate differences through communication, which is itself complex terrain. Your students will come into conflict for a variety of reasons, including seeking the attention of others, deciding who goes first or what role each partner might take on in the collaborative task, and expressing disagreement around the mathematical ideas at play. In the previous chapter, we discussed resolving collaborative conflicts, such as those around attention, turn taking, or sharing resources. Here, we focus on resolving mathematical conflict. These are substantive disagreements about ideas, and resolving them requires evidence and convincing one another.

Mathematical conflict signals that students are engaged in deep work. If you see students arguing about mathematics, call it a sign to celebrate. Then, help them learn how to disagree and convince through sound mathematical reasoning so that they can move forward. To do so, support students in using the following kinds of moves:

- State your understandings: "I see that . . ." or "I understand that . . ."
- Show mathematical evidence using pictures, manipulatives, numbers, or words: "Let me show you what I mean."

- State why you disagree using mathematics: "I disagree because . . ."
- State what you agree with and why: "I agree because . . ."
- Decide together what makes sense between multiple competing ideas. You might pose the question: "How could you decide what makes sense?" Students could choose to solve the problem in parallel and compare solutions, try multiple strategies together and then compare, or agree on which idea has the most promise for making sense and move forward with that (knowing that they can circle back if needed).

If there is a substantive impasse—bring it to the class! This is great fodder for discussion. Use this as a venue for teaching how we resolve mathematical conflict by modeling the ways we provide and evaluate evidence and disagree.

Interactions with Mathematics

At the very center of the collaborative mathematics classroom are, of course, interactions with the big ideas of mathematics. As students learn to productively and inclusively interact with one another in their classroom environment, your class will be well positioned to explore their own and one another's mathematical wonderings, questions, and ideas in deep, rigorous, and joyful ways.

As you plan to build student authority in mathematics, you will want to keep the following goals in mind:

- Invite or seize opportunities for students to pose mathematical questions that the class could investigate.
- Support mathematical argumentation and discussions.

Invite or seize opportunities for students to pose mathematical questions that the class could investigate.

Posing mathematical questions is an overlooked mathematical practice. You can deliberately cultivate opportunities for students to notice and wonder mathematically (see the Appendix for the National Council of Teachers of Mathematics' Notice and Wonder protocol and Multiplicity Lab Notice and Wonder activities). These can lead to longer explorations. If you invite students to practice wondering, *and* you take their wonders seriously by giving them time to explore their ideas, then students will wonder more and there will be more to explore as a class. It is also important to listen for the wonders that emerge naturally from investigations. Sometimes these are smaller wonders connected to specific tasks, while at other times they may be large and have implications for generalizations in mathematics. You might hear:

- "Is it always that way?"
- "So, is zero even or odd?"
- "What would happen if we tried with (triangles instead of rectangles, bigger numbers, a more complex pattern) . . . ?"

When you hear these sorts of wonderings, take them up. You might say, "That's a great question. Can we pose it to the class?" or "What don't you try it and see?"

Research Note Classrooms are characterized as much by the questions students ask as by the ways teachers answer questions. Kemmerle (2016) examined student question posing in mathematics classrooms and found that the distribution of authority among the teacher and students in mathematics classrooms affects the categories of questions students ask in mathematics lessons. In classrooms where authority is shared, students asked questions that were more conceptual, fostered mathematical connections, and built community. In classrooms where teachers held the authority, students asked questions about procedures, assessments, and meeting teacher expectations.

Support mathematical argumentation and discussions.

Facilitate discussions that expect students to explain and provide evidence for their thinking and be willing to revise it. Your job is to create a space for students to share ideas or pose questions, even when ideas are incomplete, and then reflect the ideas back to students for discussion.

Too often, students who are perceived as "smart" garner undue influence while students of lower academic status are ignored or have their ideas rejected, even when their ideas are fruitful (Barron 2003; Engle, Langer-Osuna, and McKinney de Royston 2014). To support productive interactions with mathematics, discussions should center on sorting out mathematical arguments and co-constructing new and more developed ways of thinking mathematically. Ask students, "What is persuasive? What else do we need to know or see? What's clear? What's fuzzy? How could we resolve our confusion or conflict?" For more on supporting productive mathematical discussions, see the resources in the appendix.

Research Note Coming to a New Shared Understanding of What "Good at Math" Means. Ruef (2021) describes how sixth-grade students and their teacher, Ms. Mayen, co-constructed what it means to be good at math as contributing actively to mathematical argumentation, whether by offering ideas, evidence, or questions or engaging with those of others. Ms. Mayen used a variety of strategies to support this construction. For example, students' contributions to mathematical discussions were supported in part by a "one mic" norm wherein students shared the conversational floor through a determination of who "had the mic." Ms. Mayen also introduced team roles that distributed authority to students by giving them a specific way to contribute to the work. She explicitly valued mathematical risk-taking, using language such as asking students to "be brave" and using the word *yet* to express possibilities for continued growth and learning; she also reframed what it means to be "helpful" from telling answers and explaining procedures to explaining and justifying their mathematical thinking. By centering students' ideas and promoting argumentation in discussion, she was able, over the first several weeks of school, to bring all her students into productive participation. Mathematical authority was shared by all students, and contributions to discussions were considered on the basis of their persuasiveness, rather than based on who offered them.

Rollout

In this phase, the goals require two different kinds of work. Instead of rolling them out sequentially, we think it makes more sense to work on them together, moving between them as you feel comfortable. We invite you to think about which kind of work you feel most ready to take on, knowing that you can dance between these goals as you and students build your student-led mathematical community together.

- Three of our goals support students to develop ways of thinking mathematically together. Students need tools for negotiating, recording, and sharing their thinking.
- Two of our goals hand authority over to students to lead the work of the mathematical classroom.

Building Thinking Together

After students figure out how to negotiate getting into mathematical work, we hope that there is mathematical conflict and disagreement. Mathematical conflict means that students are struggling productively with ideas and concepts and that there is some worthy work happening. That said, navigating valuable mathematical conflict requires skill, including the ability to communicate ideas, talk moves to make suggestions or ask questions, and flexibility to consider another person's ideas. Make no mistake, this is sophisticated work. Your students can do this with supports and practice, both within their collaboration during work time and in whole-group discussion. These two venues offer you two different opportunities to model and develop students' skills at navigating mathematical debate, much as they did in the previous phase (see Chapter 4).

Collaborative Work Time

As you circulate during collaborative work time, listen for mathematical disagreement, and then focus your conferring with these partnerships on making the dispute clear, providing reasoning, listening to one another's ideas, and developing pathways to work through the debate. Emphasize that what students are doing is exactly what you'd hoped: taking mathematical ideas seriously. Diagnose the core issue: Are students talking past one another, not listening? Or are they misunderstanding one another? Are students understanding one another, but simply entrenched and not able to move forward? Then consider the next steps: Would a tool, like a drawing or model, help students communicate with one another? Would revoicing help students listen? Or have they identified the central mathematical issue of the day's work and the whole class should consider it in the discussion? When in doubt, you can always ask, "What could you do to figure out which idea makes the most sense?" During this time, you are your students' coach, helping them to figure out how to enact all that you've been teaching them when things get hard.

Whole-Group Discussion

Consider a whole-group discussion an opportunity for students to learn mathematical ideas and practices while trying on and observing how those ideas get negotiated. What they see and hear in the discussion can then influence how they debate with their partners in the future.

Given all that happens in discussion, a few minutes is not enough. If the discussion is rich and you run out of time, return to it the following day before moving on. As you enter each discussion, have an idea of your goals. You may want to focus on making sense of a particular idea, sharing and connecting multiple strategies, or getting students unstuck so they can be more productive the following day. Regardless of your specific goal each day, remember that there is a deep connection between developing ways to discuss mathematical ideas in the whole group and students' skills at navigating the same work in their partnerships. Take the time to point out how the class resolved mathematical conflict in the discussion as tools for what they can do in their partnerships, too.

What these goals involve and how they look can be very different depending on your students' development and experience with collaboration. Faith and Mary approach these goals differently for just this reason, as you'll see below.

First Grade: FAITH

With young mathematicians, it is easy to default to being the person who moves the conversation along or moves conflict toward resolution, without also doing the work of coaching the students so that over time they internalize and take on that facilitative role on their own. When I confer with partners who are in conflict, whether it's what strategy to try or whether a combination one partner has created to make 20 is actually a novel one, I listen in and ask if I can revoice what each student is saying. "Jeremiah, I'm hearing you say that you've counted your groups of 10 and then your loose ones like this: 10, 20, 30, 40, 50, 60, 70, 71, 72, 73, and there are 73 pencils total. Is that right? And Melelini, I'm hearing you say that some of the groups of 10 aren't really 10 so we need to count them all one by one, is that right?" I model this first, then ask them if they noticed how I revoiced what they were saying to make sure I first understood before figuring out what to try next. I asked them if they could try this too, coaching them each through asking their partner to explain their thinking, then revoicing to make sure they understand. As I first model the revoicing myself, and then coach the partnership through doing the same, they get the opportunity to rehearse explaining their thinking multiple times. And by pausing and explaining why mathematicians do this, I support them to internalize these skills so that they can use them in future conflicts.

There are a multitude of possible next steps. I do notice, as Melelini did, that some of the groups of 10 that Jeremiah made are actually groups of 11, but it's hard to tell without recounting because the counters were in haphazard piles, not rows of 10 or 2 rows of 5. I also know, as Jeremiah shared, that skip counting the groups of 10 is going to be a lot quicker than counting the counters all one by one. But perhaps most important to the success of the partnership, I noticed that feelings of frustration were simmering when I first approached them. Neither student was feeling heard. In situations like this, I often model a curiosity or wondering stance, which can help quiet the frustration or quell feelings of being "wrong" or misunderstood. "Hmm, I wonder if there's a way we can make sure that these groups of 10 are actually groups of 10? Jeremiah, Melelini, what do you wonder?" Hmm, they say, as they look at the counters. Melelini starts fidgeting with one pile of counters, as I repeat, "What do you wonder?" I coach Jeremiah to ask Melelini, "What do you wonder?" Melelini wonders if we can make rows instead of piles and line up subsequent rows with the first one to make sure they're all 10. Jeremiah nods, and their hands are busy as they try this strategy. Before I leave, I quickly pause them and remind them that when they feel stuck or don't agree, they can first make sure they understand each other by revoicing, then ask each other what they wonder to decide on a next step!

Fourth Grade: MARY

I give students the opportunity to practice the skills of engaging in conflict when we are in the whole group in the launch, the discussion, and math routines like number talks and notice and wonders. I have charts that give sentence frames and questions to ask. The charts are in an easily accessible location that can be seen from all areas in the room, in big writing in a color that can be seen from far away. I teach these resources explicitly and prompt students to use them.

These supports are important, but I have found that their real power comes as I model them for students in conferring and one to one. I use them as much as I can, and I make sure that I model the behaviors and language: I physically turn my body, look at the chart, and read the questions just in the way I want my students to use the resources. When I look at the chart, students turn their heads to also look at the chart, too. The more I do this, the more students internalize how to use the resources and the language.

Authentically curious listening is essential to the work of this phase. In every interaction with students, I make sure to position myself as a listener rather than the person who will solve the problem. I name what is happening, revoice what I'm hearing, and prompt students to think about how to move forward. In conferring, this sounds like: "Hmm. Sounds like you two are disagreeing about the answer. You said . . . and you said . . . How could you figure out who is right or if either of you is right?" Then, I wait silently, giving eye contact to each student until someone shares a way to move forward. During the discussion, this sounds like: "Brian, it seems like you are saying that you think the answer is . . . and Hugo, you are saying you disagree. What do you think, class? Who do you agree with and what's your reasoning?" I have a lot of patience with and trust in students and believe that they will figure out how to resolve conflict, whether mathematical, environmental, or collaborative.

Another thing I do, in the discussion, is to have students list their answers. When we have a full list, students raise their hand to advocate for their answer. I tally their responses and we use that data to think about how to move forward. This positions students to reason with what the data tell us about the math thinking and work that happened that day. I say things like "Wow that is a lot of answers, what do you think that means?" Or "A lot of you got . . . . Does that make anyone curious about their answer?"

Inviting Students to Lead the Work

Being in a community isn't just about following; it's about co-leadership. Similarly, doing mathematics isn't just about answering other people's questions and waiting for the next one; it's about seeing the world through a mathematical lens and knowing you have the power to explore the questions that emerge. Having voice and leadership within the community fosters the sense of belonging that we want students to feel to the classroom, to one another, and to mathematics as a discipline. Giving students the authority to shape their environment and the mathematical work develops this sense of belonging.

When you are ready to invite students to lead the work, look out for opportunities that you can leverage to show students the authority they have and how to use it. With the environment, this would involve noticing when

something in your classroom is not working and inviting students to share how they are feeling and generate solutions. For instance, you might notice a bottleneck that is crowding the students at one table and ask them, "How are you feeling about all these kids pushed so close to your table? What do you think we could do about it?" Invite the students—not you—to present the issue to the class, and then facilitate a discussion about relocating the manipulatives or furniture. You can use these first moments to say to the class, "If you notice something in our environment that you think we could improve, tell me or bring it to the class discussion. We want to make the classroom work for all partners." Students need to see that you will take them seriously before they are likely to start making suggestions on their own.

Similarly, with mathematics, listen for students casually posing interesting mathematical questions that you can take seriously. This often takes the form of a wonder, like "Huh, I wonder if that always works . . ." that comes and goes in a flash. When you're ready to share the authority to shape the mathematical questions students explore, seize moments like this to wonder right along with students, as in, "I wonder that, too. What could we do to figure it out? Do you think others might be interested in this question? Why don't you spend some time working on that." If you want to foster such opportunities, consider using a Notice and Wonder routine (see the appendix for resources) where students are invited to wonder, often about a mathematical image or situations, without a set mathematical focus or goals. You can then invite the class to choose a wonder to explore together, or let partners each choose their own question. Students who have never experienced the authority to pose questions and have them change the mathematical work for the day will likely not attempt to do so without you opening the door in these ways.

When students do pose these kinds of questions, ask yourself:

- Do students have something to learn from pursuing this question?
- In the long run, would spending time on this question support my goals for my students, in either their identity or their learning as mathematicians?
- Can you make the time, and if so how much?

We know that there is much to do in the academic calendar, and setting aside plans for twenty minutes, a lesson, or a week can feel like a sacrifice that you cannot always make. But choosing to do so can offer big, and often unexpected, gains; these are the moments that students remember years later.

First Grade: FAITH

Our time with our students is limited, and bell schedules and transitions often seem to conflict directly with possibilities for letting students take the lead. Although not every wondering or idea gets taken up in a whole-class setting, I always try to maintain a caring and curious stance, even in the moments when I also need to name what's constraining our pursuit of this question. If I am feeling flustered or respond in the moment in a way that feels flippant, it is critical that I follow up in a genuine way, by naming how I was feeling in the moment, by apologizing, by naming what I will do differently in the future, and either taking time then or setting a time in the future to revisit the student's question, idea, or wondering.

> **Research Note** **Shea Numbers.** Deborah Ball, professor at the University of Michigan, famously took her third graders seriously when the question of what makes an even or odd number became complicated by an idea from one student, Shea. Shea contended that a number like 6, which could be formed from 2 threes, could be considered both an even and an odd number, because 3 was odd, but 2 of them—an even number—together made 6. Instead of ignoring this idea or telling the students that Shea was wrong, Ball made this notion the center of the class's mathematical debate, a discussion that went on passionately for thirty-five minutes and culminated in new thinking about the nature of evenness and oddness (Ball 1993). Ball made a careful pedagogical decision that Shea's line of thinking would generate productive debate (for more see Mathematics Teaching and Learning to Teach, University of Michigan 2010). Taking students' ideas, questions, and strategies seriously requires teachers to be willing to follow that thinking even when it is unexpected, unplanned for, and even incorrect, if the ensuing discussion might support discussion like that among Ball's third graders.

But whenever possible, if a student poses a question during a conference, or in line on the way back to the classroom from recess, about a mathematical idea that they or their peers could all gather around and learn from, I follow their lead. If it doesn't feel possible in that immediate moment, I acknowledge it directly with the student, and ask if they could bring that question to the whole class for us to investigate. One year my students organized a bake sale, in hopes that the money we raised could support efforts to reunite separated families seeking refuge at the border. It was happily chaotic, with many of our school's students and teachers buying cookies, brownies, and other treats we'd baked at home. There was a flurry of exchanges at the registers, and so many exciting questions asked as they were engaging mathematically in the moment. At one point, Erick exclaimed that we were making so much money, and what would be the best way to count and organize it at the end? Leo was working on giving change to a student who paid for a one-dollar brownie with a five-dollar bill. He counted out four dollar bills, then looked at me and smirked, "I bet there's a lot of different ways I could have given him change!" I asked, "How could you? Do you want to try to figure it out?"

These moments can be fleeting, and there will most assuredly be times when it's not possible to follow a student's lead due to constraints beyond your control. But when I engage with a caring and curious stance and facilitate that stance among all members of our classroom community, it feels more possible for students to develop authority and for me to follow their lead.

Fourth Grade: MARY

When my students have grown strong math identities, they will start mathematizing the world and advocating for math inquiries. Students will suggest tasks, situations, or context that they want to explore and, when it makes sense for their learning, I let them lead the way. Sometimes students will notice something mathematical during a science or reading block and, if time permits, I will let them follow that inquiry whether we are in our math block or not. For example, sometimes students need time during our reading block to figure out how long it will take them to read their chapter book, or how many pages they read at school and at home, and I let them figure it out. I value these moments and I want students to be making decisions about their learning. Sometimes students will be entrenched in figuring out a math task and will be lingering at their spots rather than coming to the discussion. Instead of interrupting their thinking, I ask: "Do you need more time? You can continue working at the tables or you can come back to it at recess. But we are going to start the discussion." One time, a student did this and then got really upset because he didn't want the answer to be spoiled by overhearing the discussion. So we found another location, outside of our classroom, where he could go until we finished the discussion. Being so engaged in your mathematical thinking that you see the answer as a spoiler is my goal.

I want the classroom to be seen by students as *their* learning space, not *my* classroom. To share the authority, I let students grapple with being responsible for the space. I do this by allowing things to get a little messy. If there are manipulatives all over the room or notebooks left on the tables, I don't prompt students to clean it up. I let it sit there until a student notices and brings it up. This comes after many weeks and months of teaching them how to clean the space, what the room needs to look like, and most importantly, why. We have class discussions about why our materials need to be organized or why the chairs need to be pushed in. This supports students to understand and feel responsible for the space. Some students grapple with this all year and some pick it up right away, but together we figure out our strengths and how we can all participate in creating a community that is respectful of our space.

Questions to Consider as You Plan Your Rollout

Here are a few questions you might think through as you map your own way to roll out the goals in this phase.

- What could mathematical practices, such as justification or argumentation, look like for your grade level or students?
- What are your current norms for sensemaking or convincing one another?

  - How are students already explaining thinking and listening to one another?
  - What do they still need to learn?

- Are there other times in your day when students negotiate thinking together?

  - How do they do that already?
  - What does it sound like?

- What leadership in your classroom do students already have? What skills have they learned that they can apply to the mathematics classroom?
- What language supports could you offer to help students think together? What language do they already use? Keep in mind you might hear this language at any point during your day.
- What issues could you invite students to lead in addressing? Are there any challenges with your routines or physical environment that students could problem-solve?
- What configurations make negotiating ideas easier or harder for students? Pairs? Groups of three or four? Grouping particular students?

Reflecting Along the Way

As you roll out these goals with your students, pay close attention to how things are going, your growing trust for students, and what they may be struggling with. We've found these reflection questions to be useful tools, and they can also support reflective conversations with your colleagues as you co-plan or learn together.

Reflecting on Interactions with the Environment

- Are students noticing or pointing out areas of the classroom environment that could be revised to work better?
  - Are there aspects of your environment that you see could be revised (e.g., accessing materials, sharing space, choosing places to work)?
  - How could you hand over authority to students to solve these problems?
- Are students making suggestions about how to make changes to the environment?
- Have you created time and space for students to notice, suggest, and discuss changes?

Reflecting on Interactions with Others

- How are students sharing their ideas?
  - Are they clear?
  - Are they providing reasoning?
- Are students listening to one another's ideas? How do you know?
- What conflicts are arising?
  - Are students able to move through conflict without your intervention?
  - What interventions do students need to move through conflict?
  - What might they need to learn to move through these conflicts with less intervention from you?

Reflecting on Interactions with Mathematics

- When students are debating, do they focus on *ideas* or on *whose* idea it is?

  - Do you hear any language that dismisses a student's right to offer an idea?
  - Are students considering every idea?
  - Do all students have the ability to contribute their ideas for consideration?

- Are students wondering about mathematics?

  - What opportunities have presented themselves for further exploration?
  - How have you promoted wondering or question posing?
  - What opportunities could you create to promote wondering?
  - What opportunities could you create to promote investigation of students' questions?

If . . . Then . . .

In this section we offer some thoughts on common situations that arise during this phase of establishing your mathematics structure. These suggestions are meant to be utilized as classroom routines throughout the year.

If a student's ideas are getting dismissed without consideration, then . . .

Slow the group or class discussion down and create space to consider the student's ideas. Insist that the student have the space to speak and that others demonstrate that they are listening and considering the mathematical worthiness of the suggestion. The class or group does not need to take up that idea—indeed it could be mathematically flawed—but they do need a reason not to. After attending to their classmate's ideas, students might express disagreement or offer counterarguments. However, slowing down the discussion enough to take these ideas into consideration before dismissing them is an important part of a mathematics sensemaking community. Review norms regularly that remind students of these expectations.

If one student is dominating a group, then . . .

Decenter the dominating students by soliciting ideas from the rest of the group or class. You might even point out the domination to the student so that they can become aware of how they share air time. Help the group slow down enough to attend to multiple ideas in turn. If you notice a genuine mathematical contribution from another student that the group should consider, point out the worthiness of this idea and ask the group to focus attention on it.

If students are not listening to one another's ideas, then . . .

Revoice! Model and help students practice revoicing routines. Offer language stems such as "I heard you say . . . Is that right?" If you overhear a group where students are not listening to one another, slow down their interaction and ask students to each share their ideas and revoice their partners' ideas until you know they have heard one another. This intentional slowing down can help avert moments of frustration when students feel ignored or the partnership devolving into parallel independent work. Students may, in fact, agree, but simply not be attending to one another. If you have not already, consider creating an anchor chart for students to refer to when practicing revoicing with one another. In these moments when listening breaks down, point students toward this reference and hold them accountable to revoicing.

If a group cannot resolve a mathematical conflict, then . . .

Bring the debate to the class. If students genuinely disagree about the substance of the mathematics, the issue will very likely be worthy of wider discussion. In the whole group, reframe the conflict in terms of mathematical curiosity and pose the problem as a sensemaking challenge. You might orient students to where in the task students were and then point out the differing viewpoints: "Julian thinks that this problem is multiplication because there are multiple groups. Simuel says that it is division because we are breaking up a larger number. What do you all think?" By introducing a mathematical conflict to the group, you have the dual opportunity to address students' developing mathematical conceptions while modeling how to handle disagreement and move toward resolution.

If students insist that you tell them what to do, then . . .

Students may resist holding the authority you are trying to share with them. This may look like asking a teacher to intervene on every struggle, from conflicts with a partner to deciding how to solve a mathematical task. You must match their resistance! To do so, pay attention to whether their struggle is productive. If the struggle has become unproductive, help the students anchor their thinking and get unstuck, as addressed in the previous If/Then example ("If a group cannot resolve a mathematical conflict, then . . ."). Otherwise, stay consistent in handing the challenge back to students.

Signs to Celebrate

Celebrating progress toward your goals is critical for your community to grow. Recognize small steps that accumulate into the community you and students are striving for together. The list of signs to celebrate at this, or any, stage is endless, but we'd like to draw your attention to a few signals that you might see that indicate your collaborative classroom is under construction:

1. Students have conflicts that they can move through largely independently.
2. Students are listening to one another.
3. Students are taking on the routines for sharing, listening, and negotiating with one another.
4. Students are debating ideas and not just turn taking.
5. Students are curious about mathematics and posing wonders.
6. You see mathematical practices in your classroom even without you prompting. Students explain their thinking without being asked.
7. Students talk to their peers directly and not through you.
8. Students make suggestions for how to make the classroom work better.
9. A new student joins your class and is able to integrate into doing mathematics.

6

Maintaining the Work Throughout the Year

Notes from the Classroom

FAITH: Launch Day

It's launch day of our new unit exploring two-dimensional shapes, and in addition to engaging with different tools and tasks, we're also switching up partners. In the previous unit, I noticed that all the partnerships had settled into a way of working together, and while it was our norm to choose a spot that works best for a student and their partner at the beginning of every math block, everyone seemed to be choosing the same spots each time. Jose and Allison were almost always sprawled on the library rug, Graciela and Jayden worked side by side at the blue table. But Allison was now in a partnership with Nia, and Jose's new partner was Lizbeth. We ended the launch with our typical quick reminders about how we collaborate and make plans to get started. But as soon as the students left the rug to get started Allison and Jose both beelined for the spot on the library rug, almost immediately engaging in negotiations of who would get to work there, with each of their partners protesting in their wake. I realized I needed to do more than set aside a minute of the launch for requisite quick reminders, and these new partnership dynamics required revisiting, remodeling, and repracticing how we negotiate plans and make agreements for working together.

MARY: "I Did It So Fast, Look!"

One spring, my class was busy at work with a complex math task. Lamar approached me and said, "I did it! I solved the problem really fast. I did it so fast, look!" I looked at him and then at the area where he had been working, so that I could better respond to his sharing. At his table was a special education teacher that was pushing in for support. I wanted to validate Lamar's excitement without reinforcing the idea that speed is the most valuable habit of a mathematician.

I responded, "Lamar, were you working hard to solve the problem with Ms. Rachel? Seems like you were super productive together!" Although this moment was frustrating, it wasn't unusual. Other adults were in and out of my room all the time and were bringing in their beliefs about math. When Lamar walked away, I saw him approaching several tables of students to share his success. I decided that during the debrief I would prompt the class to talk about what it means to be good at math and the habits of a mathematician. Circling back to this conversation happened all the time, but especially after a moment where a student equated success with speed, our community would need to recenter together.

Establishing a collaborative math classroom is messy work. Maintaining that work throughout the year means lingering in that messiness and revisiting goals at different points in the year as needs and challenges present themselves. A classroom community is a living, evolving, dynamic space, and there is no finality to this work. Yet as the year progresses, we can become more attuned to supporting students as they continue to build and share authority through interactions with their environment, others, and mathematics. This chapter focuses on how times for maintenance may emerge and shift as a natural part of the school year, and we offer descriptions of some signals that you need to return to classroom norms and routines. We will also discuss how different changes and transitions throughout the year impact teaching and how to troubleshoot, anticipate, and address issues as they arise.

In this chapter, we focus in particular on three times of transition that often demand work on norms and routines: (1) breaks and disruptions, such as returning from winter or spring break; (2) changes in mathematics that introduce new content or new manipulatives; and (3) changes in students, such as new partnerships or new students joining the class. These common classroom transitions can bring with them the need to refocus on some of the goals of your mathematical community. Other signals may also point toward a time to revisit, revise, or remind students of a routine: a noisy and distracting work period, a routine that feels stale, or a day when students seem stuck. In this chapter we offer ways you can address these situations.

Returning to the Goals

There are few goals in classroom life that we accomplish and never have to return to. Even when students have built skills toward a goal, they may need to relearn how to apply those skills in a new context when the situation changes.

We see three ways that you might return to a specific goal that the class had worked on earlier in the year.

1. **Revisiting** the work you did around a goal in a new context. For example, you gave students time to explore manipulatives at the beginning of the year, but when new manipulatives are introduced, you'll need to provide this exploration time with them, too. Revisiting makes sense when students have skills, but the context has changed and they need a chance to extend their capabilities into a new situation.

2. **Reminding** students of a routine or norm. For instance, after winter break, you will likely need to refresh students' memories on how to revoice or choose a productive space to work if they were already doing these well before the break, because they simply haven't done so for two or more weeks and need to get back into routine. Reminding makes sense when students are, for any reason, out of practice with skills they had already developed. They simply need a refresher to reactivate the skills and use them more consistently.

3. **Revising** how you and students are working toward a goal. For instance, you might get to a point where the table configuration in your classroom no longer provides the kind of space students need to work. They may want more space on the floor or need more room between tables to move. In this case, you may want to rearrange the furniture, revising your physical environment. Revising makes sense when a routine or norm is no longer working well for your students. Your students' needs have changed as they grow and the ways you meet your goals need to adapt along with those changes.

Anticipating the Need to Return to Your Goals

Returning to one or more goals might be prompted by one of several natural rhythms for transitions within the school year. In the sections that follow, we first focus on three times when you can anticipate that you will need some additional attention to your mathematical community: ■ changes in the environment, ✳ changes in the mathematics, and ● changes in students. In Figure 6.1 we have color-coded the goals you will most likely need to return to at these moments, but you may find that your community needs to work on other goals.

Once you have identified one or more goals that you need to return to, we suggest going back to the previous chapters to remind yourself of what tools are available to you and what you've already done with your students that you could revisit, remind students about, or revise.

Changes in Environment: Breaks and Disruptions ■

Although teachers strive to create stable, predictable classroom environments, changes in that environment are inevitable. Most prominent are changes caused by the school schedule, which can include extended breaks away from school in the fall, winter, and spring, as well as other holidays that trim a five-day week into three or four. Just as often, school events change the daily schedule, through performances, assemblies, standardized testing, or other special events that can shift how much time your class has to do math and when math time takes place. Less frequently, your students might experience changes in their physical environment, such as changes in furniture or moving to a new classroom midyear.

These changes to schedule, rhythm, and physical space often mean time away from your routines, norms, and community. Students returning from a break will need to reestablish the norms for working, be reminded of what is expected of them in a collaborative community, and practice again the tools (such as talk moves) and routines (such as returning materials) they learned earlier in the year. If you experience a change in your physical environment, the norms and routines may need to change too. For instance, where you put materials away or how you move through the classroom to do so may change with a new classroom layout. In this case, you may need to focus on revising, rather than reminding, as you create new habits for navigating your space during mathematics.

FIGURE 6.1 Goals Across All Four Phases You May Need to Return To

	Goals for Interaction with . . .		
PHASE	**Environment**	**Others**	**Mathematics**
1 **Planning for a Collaborative Math Classroom**	• Set up the classroom space so that students can access materials and resources without the support of the teacher. • Arrange furniture to support students to engage in joint work and move freely. • Set up the classroom with multiple potential math work spaces.	• Consider what productive collaborations could look like for your students.	• Select the first few days' activities that allow students to begin to engage in collaborative work and you to assess their interactions and mathematics knowledge. • Select a first unit that will allow students to do some meaningful mathematics but focus more on building interactions.
2 **Establishing a Collaborative Structure**	• ✳ Introduce the space and tools and what we use them for. • ✳ Provide structured time to explore space and tools. • ■ ● Support students to choose a space to work where they can be productive.	• ● As a class, define what a productive partnership means. • ■ ● Support students in being and choosing a productive partner. • ■ ✳ ● Support students with negotiating how to get started with collaboration.	• Begin to define what *doing* mathematics means in this space. • ✳ ● Send a clear message about what constitutes mathematical success and recognize examples immediately. • ■ Establish a clear lesson structure that includes a launch, exploration, and discussion.

continues

Changes that indicate which goals to revisit:
■ Changes in environment
✳ Changes in math
● Changes in students

FIGURE 6.1 Goals Across All Four Phases You May Need to Return To *(continued)*

	Goals for Interaction with . . .		
PHASE	**Environment**	**Others**	**Mathematics**
3 **Building and Sharing Authority**	• ■ ✳ ● Support students to choose tools, materials, and strategies that could work for them in the moment.	• ■ ● Establish routines that support students in listening to and making sense of each other's thinking. • ■ ✳ ● Redirect decision-making to partners or peers. • ■ ● Build tools for resolving collaborative conflict.	• ■ ✳ Introduce tasks that challenge students mathematically and conceptually and provoke mathematical curiosity. • ✳ ● Elicit student thinking. • ✳ ● Listen for students' mathematical intent and name their work to legitimize their ideas and approaches. • ■ ✳ ● Support students to hold the mathematical authority to resolve ambiguity.
4 **Becoming a Student-Led Mathematics Community**	• ■ Give students the tools to notice and the authority to suggest modifications to the classroom environment so it works better for everyone.	• ■ ✳ ● Build tools for co-constructing your work and thinking. • ■ ✳ ● Build tools for resolving mathematical conflict.	• ✳ Invite or seize opportunities for students to pose mathematical questions that the class could investigate. • ■ ✳ ● Support mathematical argumentation or discussions.

Changes that indicate which goals to revisit:

■ Changes in environment

✳ Changes in math

● Changes in students

Here are two illustrations of how Faith and Mary return to their goals in the wake of breaks and disruptions.

FAITH: Returning from Winter Break and the Disruptions of December

On the first morning back in January, before the school day begins, I am hastily tidying up any lingering remnants of the many celebrations and events that always seem to pile up in the weeks between Thanksgiving break and winter break. It's a reminder that although we haven't been together for two weeks, we also haven't really had a typical learning day in almost a month. Although I know I can expect a lot of excitement as we come back together and that enthusiasm will certainly carry into our work time, I can't expect that our time away and apart hasn't affected our routines, norms, and ways of working together as mathematicians. I know we will need to revisit how to build stamina for our collaborative work, pausing our work time to come together to talk about and practice the strategies and routines that help us continue our work when we get distracted or reach stuck points. We'll need to revisit how we make choices collaboratively, especially when it comes to getting started, choosing and gathering materials, and contributing to the collective work of keeping our classroom environment organized.

Right before winter break, we had settled into an easy rhythm of quick reminders from our peers before leaving the rug to begin our work. But after this extended disruption of the holidays and winter break, I knew we needed more than that to be set up for a successful work period. As we gathered on the rug at the start of our work time, there was an almost palpable buzz of excitement. I quickly explained the rules of a new task: they'd be creating a design using two-dimensional shapes that their partner would have to recreate without being able to see the original design. After a conversation where we revisited our anchor chart, I asked if a partnership could model getting started. Jimena and Sofia volunteered, and as they got up from the rug, I began to voice over what they were doing. "Ooh, listen as Jimena and Sofia are making a plan. Jimena is getting the materials they need from the math tools shelf. Sofia is getting the pens and paper. Now they have to agree on a best spot to work. Looks like Jimena wants to work at the floor table. Do you notice how Jimena is asking Sofia if she agrees? Thumbs up if you will also make decisions together by asking questions and making sure your partner agrees." I continue with this voiceover until Jimena and Sofia are settled at the floor table and they play rock-paper-scissors to decide who gets to make a design first. I turn my attention back to the students on the rug, asking if they are ready to do exactly what

Jimena and Sofia did. I more briefly voice over as the next partnership gets started and invite the partnerships to go off and get started as they feel ready. Soon, a student will take on this voiceover role, and over time we won't need this much modeling and practice every time we leave the rug to get started on our work. But when coming back from a long break, this revisiting makes all the difference.

MARY: The Arrival of New Tables

I wanted to purchase multiple round tables to support collaborative conversations and partnerships in my room, but I had to wait until I had the funding to do so. They arrived in March, when students were used to structures and routines for moving about the room with large rectangular tables. I anticipated needing to revisit and revise many things: movement in the space, the decrease in weight of the tables (they were quite light and I anticipated students would unintentionally move the tables while working), how and where students decide to sit, and the shifts in student interactions now that they would be facing each other without having to turn.

When the tables arrived, I let students know that I would need their help in negotiating the changes I just named. I used the same structures from the beginning of the year to support students to learn the new ways we would need to exist in the room. We started by having a conversation where I asked students, "What changes do you think the new tables will bring? What might we need to think about?" We talked about the best way to exit the carpet and get different materials around the room. We identified areas where traffic might build up, and we problem-solved how students should address these challenges. The conversation about how to choose where to sit and addressing the weight of the tables were easy fixes; students were equipped with reasoning skills to find solutions. They decided they would need to be more mindful of leaning on the table and if the table moved, they would need to move it back to its original spot. They didn't think the new tables would create challenges with where to sit.

The really tricky conversation happened when we discussed how they would sit together and where their materials would go because a round table doesn't have easily identified individual space. I asked the students, "At a round table, there aren't any corners. How will you know where your area is for your materials?"

The students thought silently for a while and some of them stood up on the carpet to look at the tables. One student shared, "Couldn't we have our materials in front of our chair and if they spread out too much, we could just remind our partner that we need more space?"

I asked the class, "What do you think? Will this help?"

They responded that it would help. I knew this solution would definitely lead to conflict, but I was OK with them grappling with the physical space, just as I was at the beginning of the year. Although we were in the same classroom, the environment was new for them and they would need to learn again how to use the space collaboratively.

Changes in the Mathematics: New Manipulatives and New Content ✳

Early in the year, when you began your first units, you introduced the content, contexts for learning, and the materials students might use with extended opportunities for exploration and developing norms. A shift in the mathematical content or resources can lead to a need to return to this process. For instance, at various points during the school year, you will introduce a new unit of mathematical investigation very different from the unit you just finished. This often happens when shifting from number and operations to geometry, data, or measurement. Even within a unit, you may need to introduce a new manipulative or tool, such as base ten blocks or grid paper, that can open up new strategies for solving problems or recording thinking.

In either case, students will likely need opportunities for open-ended exploration of the new tools. They may encounter challenges where they were collaborating smoothly before, such as difficulty getting started because the tasks are so unfamiliar or struggles explaining their thinking to one another because they have yet to learn the language to describe their ideas.

When you plan to introduce new mathematical content or tools, expect to devote time to exploring materials, to students planning with a partner how to get started, to eliciting student thinking, and to finding and building on students' initial successes in describing their thinking. You may notice that discussions, either with a partner or the class, become less fluid and need increased facilitation from you as students learn how to describe their thinking around new concepts and contexts. Students may also lean on you as a mathematical authority, something you will need to resist by redirecting decision-making and sensemaking to students.

MARY: Introducing Geometry and Reintroducing Geoboards

One of the first manipulatives I let students explore is geoboards. Students love to make shapes and images with this tool. I introduced them in September, and students used them outside of the math block during free time or rainy-day recess for several months before we used them to engage with mathematical concepts. We spent a significant amount of time discussing the norms for geoboards because rubber bands can be dangerous and exciting. We discussed what to do if you accidentally shoot one, and consequences if they are used inappropriately. My students became experts at using, cleaning up, and playing with geoboards.

Our first geometry unit usually happened in December. When I started planning the unit, I thought through what conversations would need to happen before we used the geoboards with a geometry lens. I knew students would need to think through how to shift the purpose of the tool.

The first day we used the geoboards for an activity, I put our geoboard norms chart on the whiteboard (see Figure 6.2) and said, "We are going to use the geoboards as a math tool. How does this change the way we use them? Do we need to add anything to our norm chart?"

Students turned and talked about the questions I posed. When they shared out, they said things like "We can't make designs during the math work time, but can we still do it at recess and free time?" I shared that as long as they were using the tool for the intended purpose during work time, they would be appropriately using the tool.

I asked, "Should we add that to our geoboard norms chart?" Students nodded and I added, "We use the geoboards as a tool in math" to our chart. I followed up by asking, "What might be challenging about this work?"

One student shared, "It might be hard to use the geoboards for math and not just for fun. Like we might forget and make a design instead of doing the activity." They were right; there were going to be some challenges shifting from seeing geoboards as a material for play to a tool for mathematics. But students had done this work before. They had made mistakes with materials and tools and knew we would problem-solve together how to be productive. Doing work with norms at this point in the year was different because students trusted me and the process more than they did in August, but that didn't mean we wouldn't grapple with challenges. It meant that we knew we could work through them together.

Geoboard Norms

* Use the rubber bands to make images & shapes on Geoboards

* Carefully place rubber bands around the nails

* If a rubber band flies in the air, say "that was an accident" loudly

* If a rubber band hits someone, say sorry & ask "Are you okay?"

* Create on the Geoboard following the directions of the task

* Make sure to return ALL rubber bands (they are a math manipulative/tool)

FIGURE 6.2 Geoboards Norms Chart

Changes in Students:
New Partnerships and New Students ●

Because collaboration is all about interaction, who students are interacting with has a huge influence on your community. When students change partners, as they ought to with some regularity, the dynamics of your collaborative classroom are going to shift. You may notice students behaving in ways they previously had not, whether they are more open and engaged or more hesitant or conflict prone. You may notice some partnerships slipping right into productive work together, while others struggle to negotiate ideas, decisions, turn taking, or getting started. Learning to make decisions with others depends on who those others are, and transitions to new partnerships can require time and support. You'll want to build in more time for these negotiations, revisit what productive partnerships look and sound like, and support students in communicating with one another and you. Even assigning students new seats can demand time to practice transitions and moving around the classroom.

Although new partnerships necessarily affect the entire class, adding a single new student can also require revisiting your goals. Do not assume that a new child dropped into your community will learn simply by watching others. Although they will certainly benefit from all your collective work before they arrived, new students need explicit opportunities to learn what it means to collaborate. Consider this an opportunity for your entire class. You might ask yourself which goals the whole class would benefit from being reminded of. Make these ideas—such as how you choose a space in which to work, how to access and return materials, what a productive partner does, or what it means to be successful in mathematics—public during a series of lessons during the launch or discussion. Consider carefully whom you select as the new student's partner. You might use this as an opportunity to position a student who often has less authority with more.

FAITH: Bringing a Newcomer into the Community

We were in the final few months of the school year, and Dalia and her family had just arrived from El Salvador. The office administrator walked her and her family over as the morning bell was ringing, and as I greeted my students one by one at the door, I let them know I'd be a minute late to morning meeting and appreciated them taking care of themselves and each other in that time. I introduced myself to Dalia and her mom, asked the office administrator if she could help me and Dalia's mom find thirty minutes to meet at some point this week, and then walked Dalia over to the rug, asking in Spanish if she would like to sit next to me. Historically, I had assigned a classroom "buddy" to a new student. Unfortunately, this would often foster inappropriate power dynamics (like the new student asking their buddy if they could go to the bathroom, or the buddy micromanaging the new student), and I wanted to more carefully facilitate the process of our classroom community welcoming a new student. After our morning greeting and our typical morning meeting topics, I asked Dalia quietly if she would like to introduce herself or if she would like me to do it. She nodded in response to the second option, and I introduced Dalia to the class and said I was so glad she was here and excited to learn more about her and from her. We ended morning meeting and transitioned to breakfast, and I invited Dalia to sit at my small-group table so that I could get to know some things about her. She loved to draw, she had an older sister in second grade, she loved her mom, and she had never been to school before. She spoke Spanish and hadn't learned English yet.

Angela came up to the table and offered to be her buddy. I decided to set up expectations for this buddy role differently, and after asking Dalia if she would like a buddy (she nodded she would), I very explicitly outlined to Angela what the role would be. She would give her a tour of the school, show her important places, and check in on her, especially during recess and lunch. "Did you know Dalia is an artist?" I said to Angela. "And she speaks Spanish, just like you!" I invited them to stay at my table and draw together on whiteboards while I took attendance. When it came time for math, we started with a number talk, where they were trying to figure out the missing number in an equation. I said the equation in English and Spanish, then as students were turning and talking explaining their strategy, I kneeled by Dalia and checked in with her. I explained in more detail what we were doing, and she started using her fingers to count one by one but still seemed confused. With very little time before I had to bring the class's attention back to the front, I voiced back to her, "I'm hearing you say you tried the strategy of counting one by one with your fingers, is that right?" She nodded. Even though she hadn't figured out the missing number, I knew this could be an important moment where I could position her as a doer of math, and when we came back together, I said, "I heard Dalia tried the strategy of using her fingers to count one by one" and prompted the class to use a hand signal to indicate if they tried that strategy, too, then named a few more strategies I'd heard students explain during the turn-and-talk.

Before leaving the rug, I wanted to revisit a few of the routines that support collaboration during work time, not only as an introduction to Dalia but also for the whole class, whose transition into work time from the rug had been slipping in recent weeks. Directing our attention back to our "looks like, sounds like" chart for collaboration, students first turned and talked with a partner then shared out what collaboration looks like and sounds like in our classroom: "We put our materials in the middle." "We make sure we agree by asking, 'Do you agree?'" "We make suggestions instead of telling, saying, 'Maybe we can . . .'" "We revoice to make sure we understand each other." "We use rock-paper-scissors to decide who goes first." I then asked if a partnership could model this in a fishbowl that I would voice over. While Samuel and Viviana began modeling, I voiced over, in both Spanish and English, gesturing with my hands to highlight particular actions that were important. I invited partnerships to leave the rug when they were ready to get started just like Samuel and Viviana, and I called out some noticings as partnerships got to work.

Over the course of the next few days, I tried to focus my efforts on doing what I could to support Dalia in learning our classroom routines, norms, and practices and looked for moments where I could publicly position Dalia with expertise and authority. When it was a routine that I knew many students could benefit from revisiting, we took time to model, collectively practice, and have discussions about how this routine supported collaboration and our classroom community. When it wasn't, I did what I could to quickly model it myself or ask a student to model while I voiced over. I also used conferences during work time to ask Dalia and her partner to share what they did or tried and then rehearse what they would share with the class. In doing so, our classroom community got to know Dalia as a mathematician, positioned as an active participant whose contributions were worthy and something to learn from and think more about. I was not perfect, and there were many instances where I wouldn't realize until we were well into an activity or work period that Dalia wasn't sure what to do. But the times I was thoughtful, and used these moments as opportunities to revisit our goals as mathematicians and collaborators, were in support of not just Dalia, but every person in our community.

Other Signals You Might Need to Return to Your Goals

Although you can see changes in the environment, mathematics, and students coming from a distance, there are other signs that may emerge at any time that you need to return to one or more goals. In this section we offer some of the more common signs along with which goals you might need to revisit, remind, or revise. However, we encourage you to follow your own intuition. If you feel like something that used to work well no longer does, try to pinpoint the goal or goals that may no longer be in hand and return to it or them. You might also ask your class to help you with this diagnosis by initiating a reflective conversation with a question like "I've noticed that we used to be able to ___ and now that seems to be hard. What do you think is going on? What could we do about it?"

If you notice any of the following, you may want to circle back to one or more goals.

A Noisy and Distracting Work Period

This may mean one of three things. First, students may have slipped out of norms for what it means to be productive and gotten rambunctious. In this case, you need to remind students what a productive partnership looks and sounds like, with specific attention to how one partnership's productivity can affect other people. Second, students may have been engaged in a naturally noisy or exciting activity, and they needed more space to spread out to accommodate this. You might then revisit how to choose a space to work in light of the kind of activity they are being asked to do. Third, students may have had trouble getting started with the activity because they were unsure what to do and then gotten noisy. In this case, you can bring all students together and discuss the meaning of the activity or support them to work with their partner on deciding how to get started.

Students Appearing to Have Outgrown a Support

Sometimes a routine or support that was needed early in the year no longer feels necessary. For instance, you may have needed to ask students to choose how to get started with their partner on the carpet early in the year, but now you think they could just as easily do this at their seats in their own time. Or perhaps you had a rotation in place for highly coveted working places, but students are no longer vying for those spots. If students have outgrown a support, celebrate their growth publicly and tell them you are retiring the routine, norm, or support because they no longer need it. Use it as an opportunity to show students their progress and revise your norms as needed.

Students Getting a Little Sloppy or Inefficient with Routines

Pay attention to what feels inefficient. You might notice transitions taking longer, materials not being put away as expected, or students issuing more commands to one another rather than negotiating. Try to pinpoint the routine that is no longer working and decide: Is the routine not working because students have outgrown it (see previous discussion), or does the routine need to be reinvigorated? If the routine needs new life, use a launch to remind students of the routine or a discussion to invite students to reflect on what might need to be revised. Bring the routine back to the center of students' attention and hold them accountable to what you know they can do.

A Low-Energy Slump

Every year includes some doldrums, where students seem slower and the energy is low overall. There isn't one specific goal, norm, or routine that is suffering. Rather, everything and everyone is dragging. This is not a moment to hold students accountable as we did above. Instead, create time in the launch or discussion to attend to one another's emotions. Notice aloud the low energy. Ask students how they are feeling. You may not be able to fix what is going on, but you can humanize students by recognizing and legitimizing their emotions. This is something we all go through from time to time, and normalizing that is a key step to making all your norms for a collaborative community feel reasonable and humane.

Arguing About Sharing or Turn Taking

You may see some bickering resurface in your class, where students suddenly seem to have friction trying to share materials, take turns, or decide who will record on a shared sheet or chart. In a discussion or launch, notice these trends aloud for students and invite them to remind one another about how these decisions get made. You may want to practice making some of these decisions on the rug before releasing students to get started on the day's work for a few days. For instance, you might ask partners to turn to one another and decide in advance where they will work, who will go first in the game they are about to play, or who will start off as the recorder. This could also be a signal that it is time to change partnerships for the entire class, particularly if students have been working with the same partners for a while. You will likely want to remind students—or have them remind you—how to share or make decisions when they switch partners (see "Changes in Students," page 136). However, a fresh start with a new partner can sometimes be a productive reset.

Marginalization of Some Students or Outsized Influence of Others

No matter how much effort you put into creating a classroom in which all students' ideas are valued and worthy of consideration, this kind of equity requires consistent maintenance. It can happen that some students' ideas are considered persuasive because of who shared them rather than their mathematical qualities. Alternatively, you may see a partnership in which one student consistently dominates the decision-making or idea generation, while another is relegated to a lower role as helper. You might notice marginalization or undue influence during collaborative problem-solving or during the discussion. In these situations, you will want to intervene in the moment to elicit the thinking and ideas of more marginalized students and moderate the domination of others. You may want to revisit or revise your routines for revoicing and deliberately elicit agreement or disagreement during conferring and discussion. You may also want to lead a reflective conversation with students during the discussion about ideas not being heard or ideas not being challenged, and then when you are facilitating conversations—either during conferring or discussion—you can deliberately elicit ideas from those whose thinking has been marginalized.

Students Following You Around the Classroom or in Some Way Demonstrating Dependence on You

Students may revert to assigning you authority that should be theirs, including asking you to referee decisions (like turn taking or who gets to hold the pencil) or mathematical correctness. They may seek your endorsement of the decisions they have made ("Is this right?") or want your praise ("Look!"). Resist the urge to praise, confirm, or take over, and instead remind students of the norms that they can and must make decisions together about how to solve problems, how to share in the work, and what makes sense. Turn their requests back into questions, such as "How will you decide who gets to go first?" or "Do you think this is right? Why?" And if this pattern is occurring in more than one partnership, revisit the norms associated with students' authority with the class in a discussion.

Students Becoming Focused on Speed, Correctness, or Competition

The gravitational pull of speed and correctness in mathematics in our society is strong. Students may receive messages that value these two qualities from home, from media, and even from one another. This might sound like an emerging competition to see who finishes first or comparing who got answers right or wrong with cheers or teasing rather than sensemaking. If you hear these messages cropping up in your class, you must revisit and remind students of what mathematical success means. Recommit yourself to recognizing publicly acts of doing mathematics that run counter to the focus on speed and correctness, including thanking students for sharing mistakes or confusions because they allow the class to learn or acknowledging students who thought slowly and deeply about a task.

Always a Work in Progress

The collaborative math classroom is something we are always accomplishing but never finish. As you notice or anticipate the need to return to your goals, keep in mind that this is both natural and within your power as the facilitator of the community. Self-reflection, analysis, and experimentation should be part of your community's weekly classroom life. It's always worth asking questions like "How is it going? How are we working together? Is everyone being heard? What do we need to work together on mathematical ideas? What challenges do we have to navigate as a community next?" Sharing authority with students is constant work, and at times this work can raise complicated feelings for teachers, such as fear of losing control, that also require careful and ongoing reflection. In the next chapter, we dig into these issues and consider how you can share authority without feeling as though you have lost it.

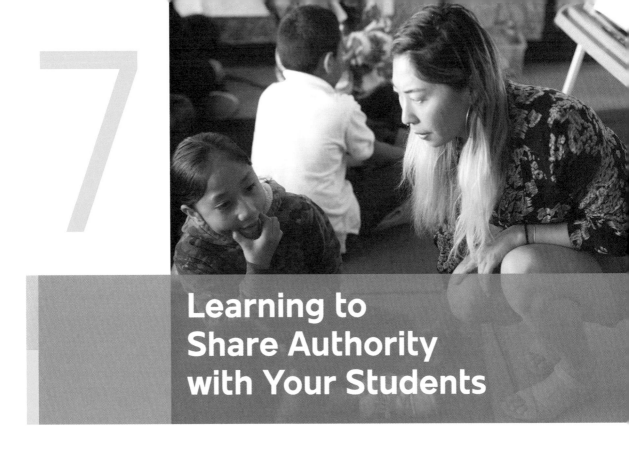

7

Learning to Share Authority with Your Students

Notes from the Classroom

FAITH: Cube After Cube After Cube

To launch our measurement unit, I invited students to measure things in the classroom with linking cubes. There was a lot of enthusiasm as they wondered if the shelf would measure as many cubes long as the table or which book was the biggest in our library. We revisited our collaborative routines, and students got to work in partnerships. Luis and Leo quickly decided to take on the task of measuring the entire length of our classroom. As they scurried around on the floor, the other students were drawn toward their work, asking questions and soon joining them. Soon they had recruited every single one of their classmates. Joanna had the idea to make same-color rods of ten linking cubes, so when they were all done they could count the cubes in groups of ten. There was consensus and some students took on the task of grouping all the linking cubes by color to make the task easier. A couple of students kept looking over at me, wondering if this was OK, as I smiled, nodded, and wondered what to do next. I was glad to see this robust display of student authority, creating something even more exciting and engaging than what I'd had in mind. But was this how I wanted them to spend their time? And what about cleanup? I eyed the clock and knew there was no way they could complete this task and count all the cubes *and* clean up before we had to line up and go to music class.

And yet, this was exactly the kind of joint work I wanted to see and redirecting the class as they were doing the task, collaboratively and with so much joy and authority, would have been counter to my goals. I decided to lean in and take on the necessary logistical role of time management and organization. I paused their work, and noted the time we had left, and that I didn't think there would be enough time to finish and clean up in time to go to music. If they wanted to continue, we'd have to take ten minutes from choice time after we returned from music to clean up. I asked if they agreed with this change in schedule and was met with many thumbs up. Maybe we would run out of time and not be able to count all the cubes before music. Maybe we would need to leave the line of cubes overnight and spend our closing meeting writing a note to the custodian apologizing and explaining our work. But they were also standing in their power and taking charge of their learning. It was well worth it.

MARY: Feeling Like Chaos

When I started establishing a collaborative math classroom, sometimes it felt OK, but most of the time it felt chaotic. It was loud; students were moving about the room and engaging in the task with varying attention; the work students produced wasn't what I anticipated. There was a lot for me to process. I struggled to feel successful and that made it harder for students to feel successful. My reaction to the environment was to freeze, unable to respond to what was happening, and ask myself, "What do I do?" But I didn't want to give up on the work.

I would stand or sit in the room with space between me and the students. I would write down my observations, so that when the work time was over, I would have data to look back on, because I knew that my overwhelmed feelings impaired my ability to assess the situation clearly. Some days, when I was really struggling, I would stand in my doorway so I would feel the breeze outside and have even more distance from the environment. My next strategy was to ease myself back into the environment. I did laps around the room looking at what students were producing, ways they were using the manipulatives, and the conversations they were having. Some days I needed to be in the doorway, some days I spent most of the work time walking around, and some days I would sit down at a table and just listen in. I gave myself permission to ease into this work so that we could all feel good in the space.

Now, I feel at ease with the sounds of a collaborative math classroom—students talking at varying levels, manipulatives banging all over the tables and floor, and students walking around the room, lying on the floor, sitting at tables, and going up to other partnerships. The student behaviors have mostly stayed the same, although they adjust and grow, too, but I became comfortable with the idea that student growth and learning are more important than my need for control over the environment. The behaviors I had labeled as being unproductive and chaotic are signs of students having authority and agency over their learning. I can look at these behaviors and see fascinating mathematics happening.

Creating a classroom where students are in charge of their own learning requires a teacher to *hold power* while *relinquishing control.* In this chapter, we describe the differences between control and various forms of authority. We then discuss the work of relinquishing control and sharing authority with students, while continuing to steer activity in ways that enable this important work. Far from a free-for-all, the collaborative classroom involves responsive leadership, shared stewardship, and understanding who students are, what they bring into the classroom on any given day, and what they need to develop a sense of themselves as mathematical thinkers and the skills and tools to productively and powerfully mathematize their world.

Control vs. Authority

The vision of a collaborative classroom that we have shared in this book is destroyed by too much control. Control and authority are not the same thing.

Control means that the teacher and the teacher alone dictates what happens, who does what, and who has access to materials, choices, and resources. Control limits students' learning because they don't have the authority to construct and test ideas, make choices, invent, and make mistakes. Control begins with a vision not of students engaging with and sharing ideas, but of specific expected behaviors and outcomes focused on performance.

In a collaborative classroom, however, the teacher has critically important forms of *authority* foundational to the work. The teacher brings to the classroom a particular vision that informs everyday choices such as: (a) what units and tasks to present to students; (b) what routines and participation structures to organize units and tasks around; (c) what aspects of students' work and thinking to highlight for a given purpose on a given day; (d) how to orchestrate classroom discussions; and, importantly, (e) how to respond to students' ideas and behaviors. This authority allows the teacher to intention-ally invite students to *share in authority* as they become stewards of their own learning and mathematical explorations. Rather than giving up power, we invite teachers to become more intentional with it, using it to shape the class-room, set the stage, and guide the ship. Not a general of troops, moving in lock-step, but the coach of a soccer team, building capacity for the players to take on the game together on the field.

There still may be times, of course, when a teacher must step in and *take control* of a situation, such as instances of bullying or other unsafe behavior. But when it comes to issues of classroom management, control is no longer at the center; instead, classroom management is reframed in terms of building an intentional intellectual community with students who each contribute to that community.

Children, like all of us, learn best when they can come to "own" their responsibilities internally and with a sense of purpose. At the cognitive level, focusing on behavior, such as sitting and practicing known procedures repeatedly as the basis of instruction, reduces the learning opportunities for students. In contrast, inviting students to think and make sense of ideas with one another creates more complex, higher-order learning opportunities that promote conceptual understanding of mathematics as well as the skills for engaging in important mathematical practices (Stein et al. 2009).

Consider, for example, the request for students to "show their work." In a controlling classroom, a student who does not show their work is punished, whether through grades or other consequences, because they did not engage in the expected behavior. In a classroom that promotes shared stewardship, you might ask a student who has not shown their work in writing to share their thinking in a different way, such as explaining it to their partner, or, if they are unsure, to ask for help, because the goal is for the students (and you!) to under-stand one another's thinking and for you to respond to it in ways that will nudge them forward ("I see that you didn't write anything down here. Help me under-stand how you got to this solution." Or "Explain it to your partner and I'll come back to check in." Or "Your thinking is really important, so let's find a way to get it out on the table for conversation."). The approach is responsive, not punitive.

The Importance of Trust

Trust is at the heart of a collaborative classroom. Although there may be a wide range of reasons why students struggle to engage in a task productively, *trust* here refers to a fundamental assumption that children are earnest in their efforts and bring a variety of assets to classroom activity that can be noticed and utilized to support moving the work forward. Similarly, it is important that students trust you and, of course, that you trust yourself and the choices you make to navigate this terrain. Part of developing trust in yourself and your students, and to foster students' trust in you, is to be consistent and clear about what students can choose, when, and why. This might mean beginning with a smaller set of choices—for example, a set of manipulatives to choose from rather than any manipulative in the classroom.

Be in the Moment

The collaborative classroom is centered around student thinking and task-related decision-making. The teacher is thereby largely *responsive* to what occurs in the moment. For example, in open-ended activity, a teacher might anticipate particular student strategies but cannot wholly predict what students might share or need to nudge their thinking forward. This requires a mindful orientation to teaching.

To teach mindfully is to keep your attention attuned to the present moment, not controlling it but responding to it. Remaining present—rather than thinking about the past or the future or something else—increases the likelihood that you can respond in ways that both accept and productively guide students' actions and interactions. Remaining present is also made much easier—and more joyful—from a stance of curiosity.

In her book, *In the Moment*, (Munson 2018) Jen identified some common unproductive and productive stances for teachers while conferring with small groups in the collaborative math classroom. Unproductive stances include:

- a management stance, focused on getting students on task and catching students off task,
- a completion stance, focused on getting students through a task to an answer, and
- a fix-it stance, focused on looking for errors in student thinking rather than understanding it.

A productive stance, instead, is a stance of genuine curiosity about students, their thinking, and how they go about engaging with one another. Mindfulness is the foundation of this work (Munson 2018).

To cultivate your own curiosity about students, actively wonder, as you look at student work or listen to students talk: What do students seem to understand? What interesting things did they try? What's surprising or confusing? From a stance of curiosity, in-the-moment teaching moves emerge, such as eliciting student thinking with talk moves like "What are you trying?" or "How did you figure it out?" (See *Talk Moves* by Chapin, O'Connor, and Anderson [2013] for a thorough guide to effective eliciting and probing talk moves.) These moves make student thinking visible, offering the opportunity to gain insight into how a student thinks about a problem or a math concept, allowing you to respond in ways that acknowledge where the student is in their thinking and help nudge them forward productively.

Staying in the moment as a mindful teacher also requires some degree of emotional self-regulation, as our minds naturally pull us away from the present moment and anxieties or frustrations tend to creep in. When you inevitably catch your mind drifting away from the present moment with students, simply notice that it drifted and come back. Similarly, when you feel emotions such as worry or frustration rising, take small actions to bring yourself back to a calm presence. For example, earlier Mary mentioned giving herself physical distance from students at times and meeting her own sensory needs with fresh air. Other strategies include noticing where particular negative feelings exist in your body—for example, you might feel anxiety in your stomach or frustration in your throat—and visualize making physical space for those sensations such that the tightness in your throat can simply be there and coexist with other bodily sensations. Taking deep breaths is also helpful, as well as other grounding techniques such as briefly naming silently what you notice in the moment with each of your five senses—I see a desk, I hear students laughing, I smell sharpened pencils, and so on. These strategies all help to ground you back into your body and come back calmly to the present moment even as difficult thoughts and feelings attempt to pull us away. Once grounded, you can make decisions as to whether to intervene in a partnership's interactions or let them resolve their differences on their own, for example, or how to respond to students' thinking in ways that might nudge them forward.

Planning to Share Authority

As you begin this work, we suggest that you let go of control and begin to share authority little by little. To gauge where to begin, ask yourself these questions:

- What forms of authority feel comfortable to share? For example, it may feel much more comfortable to share authority by orchestrating whole-class discussions based on students' own thinking, although it may remain a bit daunting to jump right into allowing students to decide where in the room to go with a partner and do some work. This is OK. As you expand your comfort zone, try letting students take on more choices. You may notice that well-structured classroom routines go a long way in making it feel more manageable and comfortable to allow students to take on more of the intellectual work.

■ What forms of student authority feel risky? For example, it may feel risky to allow students to choose which tools to use for a particular activity, as they may end up going down an unproductive path. Perhaps beginning with a limited set of options and expanding those options over time feels like a more comfortable way in.

SELF-MONITORING QUESTIONS

As you seek to let go of control over time, you are likely to notice moments when you feel uncomfortable, when it's difficult, or when you resist sharing authority with students. You can use the questions below to help you notice, monitor, and respond to these moments:

+ When do you notice you feel out of control? What is happening around you? What is happening within you? What triggers feelings of worry or upset?
+ What worries do you have?
+ What does it feel like in your body when feelings of lack of control arise?
+ What are you tempted to do in these moments?
+ What else could you try to maintain students' authority? How could you address the triggers without taking over? (For instance, if the noise in the classroom is a trigger, could you try spreading students out or developing a volume scale to use to ask students to turn the volume down?)
+ How does it feel when you bring your attention back to the moment and attend to what students are doing or trying? What are the details of student work that you can focus on instead of the triggers?
+ What helps you maintain a sense of presence?
+ What shifts when you take on a stance of curiosity?

The goal of these questions is to develop self-awareness as you engage in this process of sharing authority with students. Noticing your own comfort zone, the feelings that arise when you intentionally step outside of it, and the strategies that help ground you to the present moment will all help you develop your own capacity to create a shared intellectual community with your young mathematicians.

Research Note **Rights and Obligations.** A teacher always holds authority in the classroom, even when they share it with students (Amit and Fried 2005). One way a teacher does this is by distributing particular rights and obligations to students (Herbel-Eisenmann, Wagner, and Cortes 2010). In Chapter 5 (page 113), we shared about Ruef's (2021) study of a classroom that shared authority with students. To do so, the teacher held students accountable—a form of authority itself—to sharing their thinking, expressing agreement or disagreement, and being open to the thinking of others. Holding students accountable creates particular obligations for students that also serve as important intellectual rights— the right to make sense of mathematics, to have one's own ideas be worthy of consideration by others, and to contribute to the mathematics community.

Challenges and Ways Forward

Perhaps some of your discomfort in letting go of control or sharing authority with your students comes from specific challenges in your classroom or school. For instance, your students might speak many languages, or your students may push back on your efforts to share authority with them. Your class may have a lot of energy, or you may feel pressure to move quickly through the curriculum. These are real challenges, and they may create a sense of fear that a collaborative mathematics classroom is not possible. But we assure you, it is possible and we encourage you to push against your fears. In the following sections, we describe some challenges to letting go of control that you might face and how you might navigate them.

What If My Kids Speak Many Languages and Talk Is Hard Work?

Talk is indeed hard work, for all students, especially language learners. However, talk also supports English language development, and mathematical talk will get easier if students have opportunities to engage in it. You need both patience and persistence, along with a few strategies, to use talk to collaborate in a multilingual classroom.

- Provide a variety of language supports. You might seat students in language affinity groups so that they can use all of their language to express and explore their ideas.
- Provide sentence frames for explaining thinking or asking questions.
- Rehearse explanations with student partnerships before whole-class discussions through conferring, a turn-and-talk, or asking students to write out their ideas.
- Recognize students' nonlinguistic contributions; gestures, drawings, arrows and lines, number sentences, and manipulatives are all worthy ways of communicating mathematically.

Finally, trust your students. They often have a lot more tools to communicate with one another than they do with their teachers, and we often fail to recognize their competence at making their ideas understood. Children often feel safer communicating with their peers, because these interactions can feel less risky and formal than those with teachers. Understanding one another is a shared responsibility, so encourage all students to try to revoice for one another and ask clarifying questions. This supports them in seeing themselves, not just you, as having the authority to communicate ideas.

What If Time Feels Short? How Do I Make Sure That We Don't Get Behind?

This feeling often emerges from external mandates to cover content through particular materials. We feel the need to "get through" the next chapter, unit, or module. To combat this feeling, be clear—with yourself, your colleagues, and your school leaders—about your mathematical goals for students; the goal is not the next chapter, but building understanding of some key mathematical concepts, ideas, or practices. We encourage you to focus on big ideas, rather than a laundry list of tiny math topics, problems, lessons, or pages. Big mathematical ideas are not the kind students learn in a lesson. They take time to develop, across a unit, a year, or more, and they often encompass a host of smaller ideas. With a shorter list of much bigger ideas, you can decide what you really need to do to support students' development, which probably won't mean doing everything your curricular materials provide and instead focusing on the kinds of rich tasks we know allow for the most learning. This is an area where you need allies to support your approach or to protect you from pressure; talk with your colleagues and school leaders (for more, see Chapter 8) and see which external mandates are flexible or negotiable.

Finally, remember that you must focus on growth rather than mastery. Students will start each unit of study with a variety of understandings and they will similarly end with a variety of understandings; you will not get all students to the same place at the end of any unit. Instead, your goal is to support all students to grow from where they are. You can help others to see the value in this approach by talking about the ways in which students—individually and collectively—are growing in their understanding, rather than about who has achieved mastery.

What If I Teach Older Students and They've Never Done Anything Like This?

Remember that you need to take it slow and start from the beginning. Just because students are older does not mean you can skip or skim over the earlier phases we've described. Don't assume that students will know how to take turns, revoice, choose materials, negotiate strategies, or decide together on a place to work. Students may learn how to do this work faster because they are older, or it could take just as long as with younger students as you unravel entrenched patterns of working in isolation.

Perhaps even more important than developing the behaviors (such as turn taking and choosing materials) of collaboration is rebuilding students' mathematical identity and reframing what success in math means. Once students have been in school for several years, they have firm ideas about what it takes to be successful in math (often speedy, correct answers) and who they are in relation to that goal. One of your main goals should be shifting the definition of what it means to do math and bringing all your students into a belief that they are mathematicians with worthy ideas. Return consistently to these ideas, especially when it comes up in discourse. You may overhear students saying things about themselves that you must disrupt, like a student saying in frustration, "I'm no good at this!" or a competition emerging between partners over who finished fastest. In this case, use your authority to send clear messages about students' competence and belonging. Finally, remember that changing what it means to do math is a long journey and that the year you spend with them brings them closer to the destination, not all the way to it. This is why this kind of endeavor is always more successful when a whole school engages in it, rather than just one teacher or one grade level. In Chapter 8, we will discuss how to recruit colleagues into this effort, which can both support your professional learning and give students more time over multiple years to develop the skill of collaboration.

What If I'm Getting Frustrated and It Feels Easier Just to Tell Them What to Do Mathematically?

Time for that mindfulness! Notice what is triggering your frustration. Is it overstimulation, confusion about student thinking, or frustration that students are not moving forward in their problem-solving process? How can you take a break from the source of frustration? Are there steps you can take to reduce your frustration (like asking students to lower their volume to support thinking or telling them you need a moment to think)? Strategies like these are particularly useful if you are overstimulated by the movement and sounds of a collaborative classroom; if you are having trouble concentrating, listening, or thinking, it's appropriate to take a break or ask the class to adjust. However, if you are frustrated because student thinking isn't moving forward, ask yourself: Is this a moment to bring the mathematical challenge students are grappling with to the class for discussion, rather than trying to get students to do what you want? Remember that although it might feel easier in the moment to just tell students what to do and revoke their authority, in the long run this choice works against your goals and sends students mixed messages. Indeed, it is likely only to increase the frequency with which students ask you to just tell them what to do.

Instead, consider two key tools. First, if your frustration is stemming from confusion, say what is confusing you. It's OK for you to be confused, just as it is for your students. You might, for instance, say, "I think I'm getting frustrated because I don't understand where this 6 came from." By naming your confusion, you often find a hidden question that you could ask, such as "What does this 6 represent?" Alternatively, if you feel tempted to revoke students' authority and tell them what to do mathematically, remove yourself from the situation by walking away, if you can. You might say, "Folks, I need a moment to think. I'll be back in a few minutes and we can talk more then." We all have these moments where we are tempted to just do the work for students because we can do it faster; but that's not the point, is it?

What If I Have a Difficult Class or My Students Struggle with Independence?

Sometimes you have a mix of students who challenge your skills to establish routines and norms; they may have a lot of energy, like movement, be particularly social, or have frequent interpersonal conflicts. But a collaborative math classroom is still possible if you consider a few adaptations. First, focus on the most important and fundamental goals, those in phases 2 and 3 (see Chapters 3 and 4). Second, reframe your timeline; it will likely take longer and demand more from you to build authority and independence while maintaining students' safety and intellectual work. It may mean you need to give them shorter work times as you build stamina. Be sure to recognize and celebrate small successes. Third, distinguish between the skills and capacities that students do not yet understand and those they simply need more opportunities to practice. Finally, consider whether there are certain students who have particular needs, and whether meeting the needs of those individuals could help the entire class move forward. For instance, you may have one student who needs to work in a much quieter space, such as the hallway, with their partner, or a pair who would benefit from checking in with you to discuss their plan for getting started each day. Targeted supports could go a long way to building independence and collaboration for all.

What If My Kids Push Back, Protest, or Resist?

Recognize this response is normal. Just as it can be harder for you not to tell students what to do, it can be harder for them to figure out how to solve problems, negotiate with a partner, and persist through struggle. First, remind yourself of why you want to share authority with students and ground yourself in your vision of collaborative problem-solving. Remember also that this kind of protest is most often temporary and that, if you persist, such resistance will ease and not become a permanent feature of your classroom. Second, in the moment you encounter protests, be clear about why you will not give them the help they are asking for, whether it is telling them a procedure to solve a problem or refereeing a collaborative dispute. Finally, probe for what students really need and pinpoint what you *can* do that still preserves their authority.

For instance, if students say they don't know what to do, probing may reveal that you can support them by revisiting the task together to make sense of what it is asking or by referring students to an anchor chart of what to do when you get stuck. If you persist in offering supports that preserve students' authority, eventually they will learn how to ask for the help you will give and grow into their own authority.

What If Kids Are Confused About or Uncomfortable with How to Use Their Authority?

Encourage them to see and take opportunities to use their authority! If students ask you for permission to do things they have the authority to do, you might ask in return, "Are you allowed to get your own manipulatives?" If students are confused about what they have the authority to do or decide, clarify. Be consistent and clear about what students can choose, when, and why. Mapping the terrain of students' authority is part of you exercising yours. Finally, understand that students' hesitancy to exercise authority may stem from negative experiences in the past. They may not yet trust you not to respond with yelling, disappointment, or humiliation, as could have happened in previous classes.

In such a situation, students need care and patience, but be both insistent and consistent about what they *can* do. And be proud of them when they seize and use their authority.

What If Collaboration Feels Too Noisy or Overwhelming for Some Students?

Everyone has different sensory needs, and part of sharing authority involves respecting students when they advocate for their own sensory needs. If the student is just feeling overwhelmed on a single day, then you can grant them a day to work alone, if that is supportive. However, if overstimulation is a pattern for one or more students, you can respond by creating structures or spaces to reduce the stimulation of collaboration. For some students this might involve working with one partner instead of two or three. You might also create more sheltered spaces to work, like a nook in the classroom or in the hallway, where noise is reduced. You can also invite the class to consider how to meet everyone's needs, sharing authority with them in communal brainstorming. You might say to the class in a discussion, "For some of us it feels too noisy or busy. What could we do with our routines and space so everyone can feel productive?" In this way, individual needs are not a barrier to a collaborative classroom; they are part of sharing authority and become everyone's collective responsibility.

Collaboration Is Always Possible

No matter your circumstances, a collaborative classroom is always possible. The pathways and timelines to achieving your goals may look different from year to year, with different students or in different grades, but a pathway nevertheless exists for all classrooms. If thinking about making that vision come to life inspires you to raise your own defenses, notice those feelings without judgment and try to move through your fear. Be as brave as you want your students to be.

Just as you need to work with and alongside your students to create a collaborative space, you need allies outside the classroom to sustain your professional learning and your endeavors. In the next chapter, we consider how to talk with stakeholders—parents, colleagues, and school leaders—about what you are doing and why and how to recruit their support for the journey.

8

Helping Others Recognize the Importance of Students' Authority

Cultivating a collaborative classroom is itself a collaborative effort. Not only are you and your students working together to create a learning environment; a collaborative classroom also benefits from a supportive professional and parent community. If you are in a situation where that support is already in place, celebrate! However, you may need to make an effort to recruit parents, colleagues, and school leaders into your vision of a vibrant, busy, inventive math classroom. Many elements of such work look very different from the classrooms you and I—and the majority of the adults in your students' lives—experienced in our youth. Parents, and even colleagues and school leaders, can be resistant to change and feel skeptical of a buzzing student-led classroom. Principals may observe a collaborative math classroom and not know how to make sense of all the activity and conversation, because it diverges so completely from our shared experience of what math looks like. In fact, the collaborative math classroom might be in tension with some of your district requirements or expectations. Talking with stakeholders, such as parents, colleagues, principals, coaches, and district leaders, about your collaborative math classroom can sometimes require convincing them that this vision is research-based and critical for students' math learning.

In this chapter, we offer guidance for how to communicate with parents, colleagues, and school leaders about the collaborative math classroom you are creating. We'll consider strategies for including these partners in your vision and building buy-in, including talking about how parents can support students' mathematics at home. Along the way, remember that you are part of a long and proud legacy and are not at all alone in this work. From Dewey's seminal work on student-centered active learning in 1916 to today's continued vision for progressive education, teachers and researchers have convincingly argued and advocated for a vision of schooling centered on student experiences. In this chapter, we will consider how you can join this tradition of advocacy and help others see the importance of sharing mathematical authority with students.

Communicating with Stakeholders

Although inside the classroom you may often be the lone adult, you are never truly alone. There are many people inside the school and in your surrounding community who care deeply about what happens in your classroom. Parents, colleagues, and school leaders all have a stake in your instructional decisions. Although different audiences have varying needs, they all want to understand what you are doing as a teacher of mathematics and need to believe that your decisions are in the best interest of children's learning. They may be curious, hopeful, skeptical, confused, or worried. Communication with these stakeholders is the key to providing them with the information they need, answering questions, easing tensions, and recruiting their support. In each of the sections that follow, we provide some advice about how you might communicate with parents, colleagues, and school leaders about your collaborative math classroom in the hopes of connecting and finding common ground.

Parents

Parents' primary concern is ensuring their child's success in school, and they can become concerned when math instruction looks different from their experiences and expectations. Parents likely did not experience a collaborative math classroom themselves and may expect math to include the demonstration of procedures and repetitive problem sets. They may believe that the best measure of their child's success is the memorization of math facts and the quick recall of answers. If that is their belief, then they might conclude that the best way to support their child at home is to drill facts or use flash cards. Your role is to use the communication platforms available to you to disrupt these preconceptions, beginning with your first contacts with parents. Do not wait until parents raise questions or express confusion or concern. Be proactive and communicate your intent so that parents know from the outset to expect something different than their own experience. Your goal, then, is to give parents an understanding of what math teaching looks like in your classroom and why this approach is useful for their children, both now and in the long run.

Start at the beginning of the year, with either a letter or, if your school has back-to-school nights or other events, an in-person meeting. You likely have lots of things to introduce parents to at the beginning of the year, from the importance of reading at home to major topics of exploration. Among these, name explicitly that learning and doing mathematics is about interaction— interaction with mathematics, with our environments, and with one another. Distinguish it from the more passive, rote, and procedural work that likely characterized their experiences in school. Point out that many, many people who experienced this kind of teaching grew to dislike and even dread math and saw themselves as not belonging in math. Tell families that everyone belongs in math and that narrow ideas about what it means to do math create narrow pathways for belonging and participation, where instead we want a much bigger view of math with room for everyone. Tell them that in your classroom, how students think and reason is more important than arriving at the correct answer quickly. Indeed, you will be providing students with tasks designed for deep thinking, and for which, given enough time, everyone will ultimately be able to arrive at a solution that makes sense. Place clear value on understanding the *why* behind the mathematics, and tell parents that when we consider why a pattern or relationship exists, we have to explore, talk, explain, and show. This is why your classroom is collaborative.

Along with this rationale, be sure to tell families what math time looks like in your classroom. Explain the structure of a lesson in which you launch a task, students collaborate and you listen to and press their thinking, and the class uses discussion to explain, justify, and debate ideas. If you have time in an in-person event, you could show them a task that you did with students recently or one you will do soon and explain what kind of math thinking it provokes and what big ideas get discussed.

Finally, tell parents how they can be supportive. Remember: they want to support their child's learning, so tell them how! Point out that flashcards and workbooks are not going to help students learn how to think mathematically and can end up undermining children's sense of themselves as math learners.

Instead, the most important thing parents can do is to engage in what we think of as *recreational math* with their children: games. Parents may not understand that playing games together builds mathematical thinking, particularly in any game that requires strategy, attending to patterns or attributes, keeping score, or reasoning about probability. Nearly all games use at least one of those capacities. Some games are more obviously mathematical than others, but parents often do not see game play (unless it involves explicit fact practice) as doing math together. But games inherently involve interactions with environment, mathematics, and one another, and they are fun, informal, and inclusive. Players have to make decisions together, from who goes first to who keeps score, and they may need to convince one another of who won and why. Playing games together builds children's collaborative capacities while reasoning and experimenting. Children will often ask, "Can we play another round?" just as they might ask for another read-aloud book at bedtime. Spending time together playing games feels good and helps build students' mathematical thinking at the same time. See the appendix for a list of some of our favorite games that you can encourage families to try around the dinner table, on a weekend morning, or in a spare ten minutes.

Be sure to fold math messages into whatever communication structures you already have available. For instance, if you send home a newsletter or update email to families on a regular basis, include examples of the collaboration students engage in and the big ideas they are learning. If you have a math night at your school, invite parents to come experience a collaborative math lesson with you or create game stations where families can learn how to play a variety of games together. Or, as Faith does (see next section), play games with families as part of parent conferences. Over time, these kinds of opportunities to learn from you can help parents see mathematics differently, and they can shift their expectations of what doing math both in school and at home can look like.

Although you can expect that most of your students' parents will need and appreciate being oriented to your collaborative math classroom, you can also expect that a small number of parents may disagree with your approach. We believe that the best way to address this is with continued communication, clarity about your motivation to support all children's learning, and a positive commitment to your approach. This can sometimes feel like a tricky line to walk: explaining without being on the defensive, listening openly to concerns without feeling as though you need to compromise your pedagogy. Walking this line can be made easier with the support of colleagues and school leaders, which we discuss in the sections that follow.

FAITH: **Using Parent-Teacher Conferences**

I have never been in a meeting or conversation with a member of one of my students' families where it isn't abundantly clear that they want the very best for their child and their education. This is often accompanied by workbooks they've found online or requests for more worksheets, more homework, and more complicated looking algorithms with bigger quantities. Sometimes they ask me about how students can solve equations faster or why they don't comprehend or use the stacked algorithm or computational procedure that the family member had learned when they were in school years ago. I speak back what I hear, that they want to support their students grow as mathematicians, and I name how appreciative I am to partner with them in support of their students. I say, too, that something else that's important is that their first grader has years and years of learning ahead, and I want them to love math and love doing math for their whole education career. That, yes, it's important that they are making progress as mathematicians, developing number sense, and being problem-solvers, but it's just as important that the work is joyful.

Sometimes open-ended inquiry tasks can be difficult to implement at home, but games are accessible, challenging, and mutually enjoyable. I ask if I can introduce a few math games that we play in the classroom, so that they can play them together at home. As I explain the directions and we play a couple rounds, I quickly explain how playing the game helps students develop as mathematicians. If the students are present, I have them explain the game and play with their family members. I offer to send home the materials to play, and I encourage them to reach out if they want to learn about a different game or change things up at home. By offering this alternative, I invite family into the collaborative math work we're doing, without devaluing or rejecting their conceptions of "good math."

Colleagues

Colleagues are a crucial support whenever you set out to try something new in your practice. They can serve as cheerleaders, partners, skeptics, and allies. Ultimately, you may have at least two different goals in communicating and collaborating with colleagues, and it is useful to distinguish between these goals as you plan how to talk with your fellow teachers. First, you will benefit from having colleagues who are also working to establish a collaborative math classroom, whether they have already begun this work or want to take the journey with you. Your goal may be to find like-minded colleagues to learn with.

Second, you may want to spread this work to other classrooms or grade levels by convincing others it is worth trying. Your goal may be to recruit.

Learning Together

If your goal is to find a group of colleagues to learn with and from, begin by looking and asking around your school. Notice different teachers' classroom environments; these can serve as a clue to who has children grouped together for collaboration. You likely have colleagues you talk with about other issues of instruction. Perhaps they want to build collaboration in their classrooms. If you have teacher leaders or coaches, they could be good resources for knowing who in your building might be thinking about math teaching in this way. And don't forget to look outside your school for others around your school district who are working on establishing math collaboration.

Together you can start a reading group or professional learning community (PLC) using this book and others (see the appendix) as guides. Consider video recording your teaching and watching videos of one another's practice together to investigate how your community is moving toward your goals and what you could try next to support students' interactions. If you have the capacity, visit one another's classrooms during math time so you can serve as thought partners about how to develop collaboration. Having colleagues who are learning along with you means that you have people with whom to celebrate signs of success and to problem-solve when things are not moving in the direction you'd hoped. Furthermore, a cohort of learners can better advocate for resources from school leaders, which we'll discuss in the next section in more detail. We all need this kind of professional support system.

Recruiting Allies

If your goal is to recruit new teachers into teaching math in this way, there are several strategies that can prove effective. First, talk about your work and celebrate your students publicly, frequently, and informally, whether in the hallways, at the photocopier, or in the lunchroom. Talk about what you're trying and why, what makes you excited, and the successes you see in your students. Excitement tends to breed excitement, without any work to persuade others. You may find that colleagues become curious or intrigued and want to know more. Invite them in!

You might invite these colleagues to join your book club or PLC, or simply to come observe your math class, once you have your community up and running. For many teachers, seeing students just like theirs engaged in rich tasks, working collaboratively, and discussing ideas can be both clarifying and persuasive. If you do invite teachers to come see your math community, be sure to frame for them what you want them to pay attention to: how students make decisions and negotiate with one another, the ideas they try and generate, how they debate and come to agreement, or how understanding develops across the community. Focusing their attention on something you feel is working well and that they will be excited about can give you something meaningful to discuss afterward and avoid the sense of overwhelm that can sometimes occur when we look at a new space. Over time, by connecting with colleagues and sharing your work, you can develop a network of support that makes taking on new practices or breathing through a difficult day possible.

Mary and Faith found one another in a school where few teachers were attempting to develop collaborative math classrooms. Even though they taught different grades and have their own voices and approaches, having a colleague in the same building to talk to about their work was a pivotal support in their journeys, which they describe next.

FAITH AND MARY: How We Leaned on One Another

Initially this felt hard. We didn't have the same lunch break or any overlapping prep time. But we commuted to school together and used the hour each way (yikes!) to discuss and brainstorm. We had also seen each other at on-site professional development (PD) and leadership meetings. We noticed each other's mindset and wanted to learn more about each other's practice, which our site administrator really supported.

We watched videos of each other's teaching during a PD session and had really interesting conversations about practice. I (Faith) observed Mary's students doing things that I hoped my students would do in a few years, and some of the same routines, structures, and struggles, too. Having that shared experience watching and discussing the video made us both feel safe to be vulnerable, especially about areas where we wanted support. We always focused on students and what they were doing using a lens of curiosity, not evaluation.

That shared experience led to us joining a school-wide "buddy class" program where our (first- and fourth-grade) students met regularly. The school program focused on having students read to each other, but we also had them engage in math tasks. The fourth graders were floored by what the first graders could do and their flexibility with numbers! The buddy class program also gave us time to talk, plan, and be thought partners while our students engaged with each other. We also used each other's successes to help get support from administrators who initially thought the approach worked in first grade but not in fourth grade. I (Mary) really valued Faith's support—it is so valuable to have a primary teacher support you while trying to introduce this work in the intermediate grades! It helped me feel like my work was seen, even when I was feeling pushback from administrators and sometimes families.

Being in the minority in terms of math instruction can feel scary, especially when you have questions or things aren't going the way that you hoped they would. We could wrestle with these questions together, and it was always about the students and the math environment, and never about whether we're good teachers. Even when we weren't entirely aligned, we could come to each other with questions or as planning partners. Having a colleague to lean on and learn from is so important to staying in the work!

School Leaders

You need the support of your school leaders to fundamentally change your instruction. You will need them to know what you are doing and why, in case you encounter a parent or colleague who is vocally unsupportive. You will likely need their understanding and protection as you work through the phases of your own learning and the challenges that emerge from change. And you will likely want some material support for your learning, whether those are modest (like a sub for an hour to visit another classroom) or substantial (like new tables for your classroom). How you achieve this depends a great deal on your context and your current relationship with your administrators. However, generally, principals and other instructional leaders need to know several things before they throw their support behind you. They need to know:

1. What your vision of mathematics instruction is
2. Why that vision is in the best interest of your math learners
3. How that vision connects to the goals of the district or school and/or how it relates to other areas of instruction
4. What supports you need

In the appendix, we have provided a letter that explains this vision of math teaching and how it is supported by research into mathematics teaching and learning. You might share this letter with your school leaders to open up a conversation about your plans or to explain what you have begun trying.

Along with these ideas, you'll need to make some connection between this kind of math teaching and other work happening in your instruction, school, or district. For instance, many schools have taken on balanced literacy instruction, positioning students to act as readers and writers with the authority to do things like choose a spot to work, a book to read, or a topic to write about. If that is true in your district, you can connect this effort to having a math classroom where students act as mathematicians do, reasoning about and debating ideas, and with the authority to do so. If your district has goals around twenty-first-century skills or STEM (science, technology, engineering, and mathematics) learning, then the collaborative math classroom can be a key part of achieving those goals. Position your new approach to teaching mathematics as a natural fit with or extension of the work already underway and you will be more likely to receive support.

Finally, if you want support, you need to explicitly ask for it. You might need professional texts, manipulatives, time to meet or plan with colleagues, or access to a conference or external PD opportunities. You may want to start a book club or PLC (see earlier discussion) and need the principal to allow space or time for gathering. You may even want your school leaders to join the work or advertise it among the faculty. Or, more modestly but equally important, you may simply want your school leaders' grace and protection as you try something new. You may want to acknowledge that no shift in practice is completely smooth and ask for the freedom to experiment. You may also want some latitude to diverge from curricula, pacing guides, or other policies as you work to establish a collaborative math classroom.

Over time, we encourage you to stay in communication with your school leaders. Share your successes and update them as you move forward. And continue to ask for support as your needs change. It may be tempting at times to enter your classroom and close the door behind you, but avoiding including your school leaders only makes you more vulnerable and less supported. Remember, recruiting your principal's support is easier to do as a group of teachers than as a solo endeavor. Gather your interested colleagues and start a conversation.

MARY: Inviting the Principal in Through a Formal Observation

One year I decided to take the risk of doing my formal observation around math. I knew my principal had limited knowledge around what constitutes success in a collaborative math classroom, but I did it anyway. This was risky because I was using my formal observation as an opportunity for her to be a learner. However, I really wanted to show my leader what strong mathematics instruction looks like. I knew that if I got her on board, it might cultivate more learning for the teachers on my campus. And I was really proud of the work my fourth-grade students were doing. During the observation, I noticed her furrowed brow and wondered if I had made a mistake. Was she not seeing the students being successful? I saw her jotting down notes and again, I wondered if her observations were a sign of disapproval. When we sat down in her office to talk about the lesson, she looked at me with a big smile and said, "Wow, there was so much going on in your room!" Our conversation ended up being more of her asking me questions and pondering what all this means for instruction across the site and how she might help other folks explore this new approach. It was a productive conversation and I was able to position myself as a leader because I was willing to be vulnerable about my instruction and practice.

Building a Broader Professional Community to Nurture You

Although colleagues in your school building are crucial because they understand your context and they can be there for the day-to-day ups and downs, you also need a broader professional community as you work to create a collaborative math classroom. Broader communities include teachers and leaders outside of your school or district who can provide inspiration, ideas, and encouragement. This is the community you go to when you need to feel connected to something bigger than one classroom or one school. A broader community can offer you a glimpse into what others are trying, how it's going, and what's possible.

There are teachers all over the world working to develop rich mathematical classrooms where discourse and ideas flourish. You might find these folks on social media, at conferences, or in PD experiences. You might even find them in books (we're here for you!). Get out there and find your people! Try exploring and participating in the math education community on Twitter (#mtbos) or look for a Math Circle near you (https://mathcircles.org/) where you can meet other math teachers in your area. Go to a conference like the National Council of Teachers of Mathematics (https://www.nctm.org/conferencespd/) annual or regional meetings or the National Council of Supervisors of Mathematics (https://www.mathedleadership.org/) annual conference, which is especially good for school leaders and coaches. Many state-level mathematics teacher organizations also host annual conferences that can be easier to travel to and get funding to attend. Talk to your school leaders about PD funds and see what is possible. If funding is an issue, some conferences have scholarships for teachers and some schools have parent organizations that will fund some PD for teachers. Consider taking a friend, coach, colleague, or principal along with you. Look for high-quality PD opportunities near you or online, and talk to those who also show up. Plus, see the appendix for more members of this big community who have written about math classrooms like those we've created, learned from, and described here.

There will come a moment when you feel flat. Perhaps you'll be struggling to fulfill your vision of a collaborative math classroom, or you'll be in the doldrums of February, seemingly forever from a much-needed break. You may simply feel uninspired or stuck in a rut. When that day comes, you need a community you can count on to jump-start your passion, inspire creativity, and inject some energy into your work. We encourage you to think generously about who you can call part of your community and who you can call on in those moments, whether it's an email to a friend, a tweet for help, or a book you can revisit.

MARY: Using Summer Professional Development to Build Community

In my second year of teaching, I attended PD to support my math instruction. At the time, I had a clear pedagogical stance, but I wasn't sure how to implement the environment I learned about in my credential program. I have attended the same regional mathematics PD institute almost every summer since then, supported by my district, which offered to send interested teachers. For the first few years, I was building and deepening my content knowledge. But as time went on, I continued to participate because it helped me to feel centered in a community of learning with people who had shared values. I started to build relationships with the facilitators that led to deepening my practice in a way that I hadn't anticipated. I was able to observe classrooms in other districts and learn about different ways to build a math community. I presented at conferences and, in these spaces, deepened my relationships with colleagues. I was able to grow a community of support that I didn't have on my campus every day. Those same colleagues are the people I reach out to when I'm grappling with something or want to engage in a book study. These relationships have kept me in the work and helped me to stay in a learner mindset. I am grateful for the opportunity to have a consistent landing space for learning.

Final Thoughts

Creating a collaborative math classroom is engaging, ambitious, and often joyful work. We hope you feel inspired and supported to get started. You will need support beyond this book as you travel this path. Collaborating with colleagues or other teachers, finding online resources or PD opportunities, and seeking support from your school leaders are all important elements. This is slow, deep work, and you will develop your skills and understanding of collaborative mathematics classrooms over time, as you try new things out and see what works, what doesn't, and where you can go deeper over the years. We welcome you to the community of ambitious math educators and hope you stay with us for the long haul!

Appendices

A Guiding Letter for School Leaders

Dear School Leader,

You are reading this letter for a wonderful reason—teachers at your school or district are interested in creating robust, inclusive collaborative mathematics classrooms. We are a team of university researchers and classroom teachers and the authors of the book *The Collaborative Math Classroom*, which offers a vision and guide for ambitious instruction in elementary mathematics.

Why collaborative math teaching?

When we imagine a mathematics classroom, certain elements are likely to come to mind: a teacher at the front of the room presenting and explaining procedures, students raising their hands if they have a question or to share the answer on individual assignments. In our book, we offer an alternative vision for a collaborative mathematics classroom. The role of teacher is not so much to explain as it is to curate and facilitate rich mathematical experiences that students engage in with one another. Students' mathematical thinking drives the day's work; teachers elicit, probe, and help to nudge students' thinking; wonder along with students; and help to create a classroom where students feel seen and heard as mathematical thinkers, learners, and community members (Gargroetzi in press).

Students in collaborative math classrooms make sense of mathematics. By exploring and investigating big ideas, such as place value, addition and subtraction, fractions, or shapes, students have the opportunity to reason with one another and develop conceptual understanding. For example, students might add two numbers by first building ten-sticks out of linking cubes and discussing what happens when the remaining ones of each addend are joined together, creating a new ten-stick. These students have the opportunity not simply to memorize addition facts, but to explore what place value is by constructing tens out of ones and reasoning about what it means to join two quantities through the mathematical act of addition. Students are able to see addition, investigate quantity, and make sense of place value.

Collaborative mathematics classrooms are not only more engaging and student centered; this approach has been shown both to increase mathematics achievement and work against inequities (Boaler and Staples 2008). Previous research on collaborative and cooperative learning has shown that students learn more when they work together on mathematics (Barron 2000; Capar and Tarim 2015; DesLauriers, Schelew, and Wieman 2011; Díez-Palomar et al. 2021). A meta-analysis of research on cooperative mathematics learning across prekindergarten through university level found that students working together increased student achievement when compared with traditional methods where instruction is teacher led and students work individually (Capar and Tarim 2015).

A key component of successful collaborative learning is that students are given agency within the classroom to use their own ideas and resources to make sense of and solve problems (Engle and Conant 2002). This requires a significant departure from the typical passive style of engagement from students in traditional lecture-style classrooms. This departure makes particular core demands of the teacher. Teachers will need you to support:

- **Local control of curriculum.** Teachers need to be flexible users of curricular material, adapting them to support student exploration and discussion. For example, teachers need to be released from top-down control such as pacing guides and mandated curriculum that stifles their ability to be responsive to the needs of the children in their classroom.
- **Teacher-facilitated professional learning communities and opportunities for teachers to visit one another and co-plan/debrief.** Teachers develop the skills needed to plan and launch open tasks, make sense of student work, and share strategies that work when they are in collaboration with one another.
- **Coaching opportunities with a district coach with this vision.** If possible, a district coach with skills in facilitating math classroom discussions and group work would go far in supporting teachers' development of skills and strategies to create and maintain robust and productive collaborative math classrooms.
- **A lens for looking: guiding questions for when you enter a collaborative math classroom.** Teachers routinely have school leaders or other outsiders join their classroom for observation and, at times, evaluation. Developing a lens or rubric for understanding the markers of success in a student-led, collaborative environment is necessary to be able to notice, name, and support what goes well in such a classroom and what aspects need support.

If you are a school leader—a principal, district official, or superintendent—it is important that you understand how to create the conditions for teachers to develop a stance of genuine curiosity about their students' thinking and to create a classroom culture that fosters children's own curiosity about mathematics. To do so, teachers need the intellectual autonomy to navigate their classrooms with their students and to collaborate with their teacher colleagues in teacher-led collaborative professional development contexts.

We invite you to learn more by reading our book *The Collaborative Math Classroom*. In it, you will gain an in-depth look at how to create such classrooms at the elementary level and what to expect as teachers begin the work to do so. We hope you are curious and perhaps even excited about this opportunity.

All the best,

Jen Munson, Jennifer M. Osuna, Faith Kwon, and Mary Trinkle

Authors, *The Collaborative Math Classroom*

*references attached

REFERENCES

Barron, B. 2000. "Achieving Coordination in Collaborative Problem-Solving Groups." *Journal of the Learning Sciences* 9 (4): 403–36.

Boaler, J., and M. Staples. 2008. "Creating Mathematical Futures Through an Equitable Teaching Approach: The Case of Railside School." *Teachers College Record* 110 (3): 608–45.

Capar, G., and K. Tarim. 2015. "Efficacy of the Cooperative Learning Method on Mathematics Achievement and Attitude: A Meta-Analysis Research." *Educational Sciences: Theory and Practice* 15 (2): 553–59.

Deslauriers, L., E. Schelew, and C. Wieman. 2011. "Improved Learning in a Large-Enrollment Physics Class." *Science* 332 (6031): 862–64.

Díez-Palomar, J., M. C. E. Chan, D. Clarke, and M. Padrós. 2021. "How Does Dialogical Talk Promote Student Learning During Small Group Work? An Exploratory Study." *Learning, Culture and Social Interaction* 30: 100540.

Engle, R. A., and F. R. Conant. 2002. "Guiding Principles for Fostering Productive Disciplinary Engagement: Explaining an Emergent Argument in a Community of Learners Classroom." *Cognition and Instruction* 20 (4): 399–483. https://doi.org/10.1207/S1532690XCI2004

Additional Resources

As we have worked to grow our own collaborative mathematics classrooms and to support other teachers to do the same, we have drawn on a variety of resources for rich mathematical tasks and to investigate how to facilitate rich talk. Below are some of our favorites that we encourage you to explore as they meet your needs.

Resources for Rich Tasks and Routines

Rich tasks

- Lilburn, P., and A. Ciurak. 2010. *Investigations, Tasks, and Rubrics to Teach and Assess Math, Grades 1–6.* Sausalito, CA: Math Solutions.
- Small, M. 2020. *Good Question: Great Ways to Differentiate Mathematics Instruction in the Standards-Based Classroom,* 4th edition. New York: Teachers College Press.
- Sullivan, P., and P. Lilburn. 2020. *Good Questions for Math Teaching: Why Ask Them and What to Ask, Grades K–6,* 2nd edition. Portsmouth, NH: Heinemann.
- Multiplicity Lab at https://multiplicitylab.northwestern.edu/
- YouCubed at www.youcubed.org

Units of instruction

- Boaler, J., J. Munson, and C. Williams. 2017–2021. Mindset Mathematics series, Grades K–8. Hoboken, NJ: Jossey-Bass.
- Fosnot, C. 2007–2008. Contexts for Learning Mathematics series. Portsmouth, NH: Heinemann.
- Lampert, M. 2003. *Teaching Problems and the Problems of Teaching.* New Haven, CT: Yale University Press.

Notice and Wonder routine and tasks

- National Council of Teachers of Mathematics at https://www.nctm.org/noticeandwonder/
- Multiplicity Lab at https://multiplicitylab.northwestern.edu/project_category/noticewonder/

Resources for modifying tasks

- Zager, T. 2017. *Becoming the Math Teacher You Wish You'd Had.* Portland, ME: Stenhouse.
- Sullivan, P., and P. Lilburn. 2002. *Good Questions for Math Teaching: Why Ask Them and What to Ask, Grades K–6.* Math Solutions.

Professional Texts on Facilitating Mathematics Talk

Resources on eliciting student thinking

- Chapin, S. H., C. O'Connor, and N. Anderson. 2013. *Talk Moves: A Teacher's Guide for Using Classroom Discussions in Math, Grades K–6.* (3rd edition). Sausalito, CA: Math Solutions.
- Kazemi, E., and A. Hintz. 2014. *Intentional Talk: How to Structure and Lead Productive Mathematical Discussions.* Portland, ME: Stenhouse.
- Munson, J. 2018. *In the Moment: Conferring in the Elementary Math Classroom.* Portsmouth, NH: Heinemann.

Resources for facilitating discussion

- Chapin, S. H., M. C. O'Connor, and N. C. Anderson. 2009. *Classroom Discussions: Using Math Talk to Help Students Learn, Grades K–6.* Sausalito, CA: Math Solutions.
- Featherstone, H., S. Crespo, L. Jilk, J. Oslund, A. N. Parks, and M. Wood. 2011. *Smarter Together: Collaboration and Equity in the Elementary Mathematics Classroom.* Reston, VA: NCTM.
- Kazemi, E., and A. Hintz. 2014. *Intentional Talk: How to Structure and Lead Productive Mathematical Discussions.* Portland, ME: Stenhouse.
- Kelemanik, G., A. Lucenta, and S. J. Creighton. 2016. *Routines for Reasoning: Fostering the Mathematical Practices in All Students.* Portsmouth, NH: Heinemann.
- O'Connell, S., and J. SanGiovanni. 2013. *Putting the Practices into Action: Implementing the Common Core Standards for Mathematical Practice, K–8.* Portsmouth, NH: Heinemann.

Math Games for School and Home

This is just a small slice of the wonderful games available that can engage students in mathematical thinking and practices through play.

- Tenzi
- Tiny Polka Dots
- Yamslam
- Blink
- Set
- Qwirkle
- Blockus

- Over Under
- Otrio
- Suspend
- Skiwampus
- Sixstix
- Battleship

References

Amit, M., and M. N. Fried. 2005. "Authority and Authority Relations in Mathematics Education: A View from an 8th Grade Classroom." *Educational Studies in Mathematics* 58 (2): 145–68.

Anthony, G., R. Averill, and M. Drake. 2018. "Occasioning Teacher-Educators' Learning Through Practice-Based Teacher Education." *Mathematics Teacher Education and Development* 20 (3): 4–19.

Ball, D. L. 1993. "With an Eye on the Mathematical Horizon: Dilemmas of Teaching Elementary School Mathematics." *Elementary School Journal* 93 (4): 373–97.

Barron, B. 2000. "Achieving Coordination in Collaborative Problem-Solving Groups." *Journal of the Learning Sciences* 9 (4): 403–36.

Barron, B. 2003. "When smart groups fail." *Journal of the Learning Sciences* 12 (3): 307–359. https://doi.org/10.1207/S15327809JLS1203

Boaler, J. 2012. "Timed Tests and the Development of Math Anxiety." *Education Week*. July 3. http://www.edweek.org/ew/articles/2012/07/03/36 boaler.h31.html?tkn=VOQFK9Wqv/QyFHqgUJA20N6MixLTNTr2KA /y&cmp=clp-edweek.

Boaler, J., J. Munson, and C. Williams. 2018. *Mindset Mathematics: Grade 3.* Hoboken, NJ: Jossey-Bass.

Boaler, J., J. Munson, and C. Williams. 2022. *Mindset Mathematics: Grade 2.* Hoboken, NJ: Jossey-Bass.

Boaler, J., and M. Staples. 2008. "Creating Mathematical Futures Through an Equitable Teaching Approach: The Case of Railside School." *Teachers College Record* 110 (3): 608–45.

Capar, G., and K. Tarim. 2015. "Efficacy of the Cooperative Learning Method on Mathematics Achievement and Attitude: A Meta-Analysis Research." *Educational Sciences: Theory and Practice* 15 (2): 553–59.

Chapin, S. H., C. O'Connor, and N. Anderson. 2013. *Talk Moves: A Teacher's Guide for Using Classroom Discussions in Math, Grades K–6.* (3rd edition). Sausalito, CA: Math Solutions.

Cobb, P. 1995 "Mathematical learning and small-group interaction: Four case studies." In *The emergence of mathematical meaning: Interaction in classroom cultures*, edited by P. Cobb and H. Bauersfeld, 25–129. New York: Routledge.

Cohen, E. G. and R. A. Lotan. 2014. *Designing Groupwork: Strategies for the Heterogeneous Classroom.* New York: Teachers College Press.

Common Core Standards Writing Team, 2013. *Progressions for the Common Core State Standards in Mathematics.* Tucson, AZ: Institute for Mathematics Education, University of Arizona.

Desautel, D. 2009. "Becoming a Thinking Thinker: Metacognition, Self-Reflection, and Classroom Practice." *Teachers College Record* 111 (8): 1997–2020.

Deslauriers, L., E. Schelew, and C. Wieman. 2011. "Improved Learning in a Large-Enrollment Physics Class." *Science* 332 (6031): 862–64.

Dewey, J. 1916. *Democracy and Education.* New York: The Macmillan Company.

Díez-Palomar, J., M. C. E. Chan, D. Clarke, and M. Padrós. 2021. "How Does Dialogical Talk Promote Student Learning During Small Group Work? An Exploratory Study." *Learning, Culture and Social Interaction* 30: 100540.

Engle, R. A., and F. R. Conant. 2002. "Guiding Principles for Fostering Productive Disciplinary Engagement: Explaining an Emergent Argument in a Community of Learners Classroom." *Cognition and Instruction* 20 (4): 399–483. https://doi.org/10.1207/S1532690XCI2004

Engle, R. A., J. M. Langer-Osuna, and M. McKinney de Royston. 2014. "Toward a Model of Influence in Persuasive Discussions: Negotiating Quality, Authority, Privilege, and Access Within a Student-Led Argument." *Journal of the Learning Sciences* 23 (August): 245–268. https://doi.org/10.1080/10508406.2014.883979

Enyedy, N., L. Rubel, V. Castellón, S. Mukhopadhyay, I. Esmonde, and W. Secada. 2008. "Revoicing in a Multilingual Classroom." *Mathematical Thinking and Learning* 10 (2): 134–62.

Featherstone, H., S. Crespo, L. Jilk, J. A. Oslund, A. N. Parks, and M. B. Wood. 2011. *Smarter Together! Collaboration and Equity in the Elementary Math Classroom.* Reston, VA: National Council of Teachers of Mathematics.

Fosnot, C. 2008. *Contexts for Learning Mathematics: Bunk Beds and Apple Boxes.* Portsmouth, NH: Heinemann.

Gargroetzi, E. (In press). "Fragile Dignity in a Mathematics Classroom World: An Ethno-Interactional Analysis of the Construction of Mathematical Competence with Dignity in One High School Math Classroom." *Cognition and Instruction.*

Grossman, P., K. Hammerness, and M. McDonald. 2009. "Redefining Teaching, Re-Imagining Teacher Education." *Teachers and Teaching: Theory and Practice* 15 (2): 273–89.

Herbel-Eisenmann, B., D. Wagner, and V. Cortes. 2010. "Lexical Bundle Analysis In Mathematics Classroom Discourse: The Significance of Stance." *Educational Studies in Mathematics* 75 (1): 23–42.

Jackson, K., E. Shahan, L. K. Gibbons, and P. Cobb. 2012. "Launching Complex Tasks." *Mathematics Teaching in the Middle School* 18 (1): 24–29.

Kazemi, E. and A. Hintz. 2014. *Intentional Talk: How to Promote and Lead Productive Mathematical Discussions.* Portland, ME: Stenhouse.

Kemmerle, M. 2016. "Questions About Questions: Promoting Productive Mathematical Questions from Middle School Students" (doctoral dissertation, Stanford University).

Langer-Osuna, J. M. 2011. "How Brianna Became Bossy and Kofi Came Out Smart: Understanding the Trajectories of Identity and Engagement for Two Group Leaders in a Project-Based Mathematics Classroom." *Canadian Journal of Science, Mathematics and Technology Education* 11 (3): 207–25.

———. 2015. "From getting "fired" to becoming a collaborator: A case of the coconstruction of identity and engagement in a project-based mathematics classroom." *Journal of the Learning Sciences* 24 (1): 53-92.

———. 2016. The social construction of authority among peers and its implications for collaborative mathematics problem-solving. *Mathematical Thinking and Learning* 18 (2): 107–124.

———. 2018. "Exploring the Central Role of Student Authority Relations in Collaborative Mathematics." *ZDM* 50 (6): 1077–87.

Langer-Osuna, J. M., and M. A. Avalos. 2015. "'I'm Trying to Figure This Out. Why Don't You Come Up Here?': Heterogeneous Talk and Dialogic Space in a Mathematics Discussion." *ZDM* 47 (7): 1313–22.

Langer-Osuna, J. M., E. Gargroetzi, J. Munson, and R. Chavez. 2020. "Exploring the Role of Off-Task Activity on Students' Collaborative Dynamics." *Journal of Educational Psychology* 112 (3): 524–32.

Langer-Osuna, J. M. and J. Munson. Under review. "Exploring what teachers notice about students' interactional dynamics during collaborative mathematics problem-solving and their connections to instructional practice."

Lerman, S. 2000. "The Social Turn in Mathematics Education Research." In *Multiple Perspectives on Mathematics Teaching and Learning*, edited by J. Boaler, 19–44. Westport, CT: Praeger.

Mathematics Teaching and Learning to Teach, University of Michigan. 2010. "SeanNumbers-Ofala." http://hdl.handle.net/2027.42/65013

McClain, K., and P. Cobb. 2001. "An Analysis of Development of Sociomathematical Norms in One First-Grade Classroom." *Journal for Research in Mathematics Education* 32 (3): 236–66.

Mercer, N., and C. Howe. 2012. "Explaining the Dialogic Processes of Teaching and Learning: The Value and Potential of Sociocultural Theory." *Learning, Culture and Social Interaction* 1 (1): 12–21.

Mercer, N., R. Wegerif, and L. Dawes. 1999. "Children's Talk and the Development of Reasoning in the Classroom." *British Educational Research Journal* 25 (1): 95–111.

Moschkovich, J. 1999. "Supporting the Participation of English Language Learners in Mathematical Discussions." *For the Learning of Mathematics* 19 (1): 11–19.

———, ed. 2010. *Language and Mathematics Education: Multiple Perspectives and Directions for Research.* Charlotte, NC: Information Age Publishing.

Munson, J. 2018. *In the Moment: Conferring in the Elementary Math Classroom.* Portsmouth, NH: Heinemann.

Nathan, M. J., and E. J. Knuth. 2003. "A Study of Whole Classroom Mathematical Discourse and Teacher Change." *Cognition and Instruction* 21 (2): 175–207.

National Academies of Sciences, Engineering, and Medicine. 2018. *How People Learn II: Learners, Contexts, and Cultures.* Washington, DC: National Academies Press.

National Council of Teachers of Mathematics. 2014. *Principles to actions: Ensuring mathematical success for all.* Reston VA: NCTM.

National Governors Association Center for Best Practices and Council of Chief State School Officers. 2010. *Common Core State Standards for Mathematics.* Washington, DC: National Governors Association Center for Best Practices, Council of Chief State School Officers.

National Research Council. 1999. *How People Learn: Bridging Research and Practice.* Washington, DC: National Academies Press.

Parrish, S. 2010. "*Number talks: Helping children build mental math and computation strategies, grades K-5.*" Sausalito, CA: Math Solutions.

Ruef, J. 2021. "How Ms. Mayen and Her Students Co-Constructed Good-at-Math." *Journal for Research in Mathematics Education* 52 (2): 152–88.

Seeley, C. L. 2015. *Faster Isn't Smarter: Messages About Math, Teaching, and Learning in the 21st Century.* (2nd edition) Sausalito, CA: Math Solutions.

Stein, M. K., R. A. Engle, M. S. Smith, and E. K. Hughes. 2008. "Orchestrating Productive Mathematical Discussions: Five Practices for Helping Teachers Move Beyond Show and Tell." *Mathematical Thinking and Learning* 10 (4): 313–40.

Stein, M. K., and M. S. Smith. 1998. "Mathematical tasks as a framework for reflection: From research to practice." *Mathematics Teaching in the Middle School* 3 (4): 268–275.

Smith, M., and M. K. Stein. 2011. *Five Practices for Orchestrating Productive Mathematical Discussion.* Reston, VA: National Council of Teachers of Mathematics.

Stein, M. K., M. S. Smith, M. A. Henningsen, and E. A. Silver. 2009. *Implementing Standards-Based Math Instruction: A Casebook for Professional Development.* New York: Teachers College Press.

Turner, E., H. Dominguez, L. Maldonado, and S. Empson. 2013. "English Learners' Participation in Mathematical Discussion: Shifting Positionings and Dynamic Identities." *Journal for Research in Mathematics Education* 44 (1): 199–234.

Walshaw, M., and G. Anthony. 2008. "The Teacher's Role in Classroom Discourse: A Review of Recent Research into Mathematics Classrooms." *Review of Educational Research* 78 (3): 516–51.

Webb, N. M. 2009. "The Teacher's Role in Promoting Collaborative Dialogue in the Classroom." *The British Journal of Educational Psychology* 79 (1): 1–28. https://doi.org/10.1348/000709908X380772

Webb, N. M., M. L. Franke, M. Ing, A. Chan, T. De, D. Freund, and D. Battey. 2008. "The role of teacher instructional practices in student collaboration." *Contemporary Educational Psychology* 33 (3): 360–381. https://doi.org/10.1016/j.cedpsych.2008.05.003

Wood, M. B. 2013. "Mathematical Micro-Identities: Moment-to-Moment Positioning and Learning in a Fourth-Grade Classroom." *Journal for Research in Mathematics Education* 44 (5): 775. https://doi.org/10.5951/jresematheduc.44.5.0775

Woodward, J., and K. Irwin. 2005. "Language Appropriate for the New Zealand Numeracy Project." In *Proceedings of the 28th Annual Conference of the Mathematics Education Research Group of Australasia*, edited by P. Clarkson, et al., 799–806.

Yackel, E., and P. Cobb. 1996. "Sociomathematical Norms, Argumentation, and Autonomy in Mathematics." *Journal for Research in Mathematics Education* 27 (4): 458–477.